Universitext

William R. Fuller

FORTRAN
Programming
A Supplement
for Calculus Courses

Springer-Verlag
New York Heidelberg Berlin

William R. Fuller

Department of Mathematics
Purdue University
West Lafayette, IN 47907

AMS Subject Classifications: 26-01, 68-01

Library of Congress Cataloging in Publication Data

Fuller, William Richard, 1920–
    FORTRAN programming.

    (Universitext)
    Includes index.
    1. Calculus—Data processing.   2.   FORTRAN (Computer
program language)   I.   Title.
QA303.F963   515'.028'5   77-12129
ISBN 0-387-90283-X

© 1977 by Springer-Verlag, New York Inc.

Printed in the United States of America.

9   8   7   6   5   4   3   2   1

ISBN 0-387-90283-X   Springer-Verlag   New York
ISBN 3-540-90283-X   Springer-Verlag   Berlin   Heidelberg

Foreword to the instructor

Five hundred years ago, some generals held the theory that the invention of artillery had made the foot soldier obsolete. The famous renaissance thinker, Nicolo Machiavelli argued[1] that artillery merely influenced the tactics which a prudent general employed. How well history had borne out Machiavelli's contention can be easily judged.

Currently, beginning calculus students frequently give the impression that they believe that the computer has made the traditional calculus course obsolete. This is not the case and there is no immediate prospect that it will become the case. However, to ignore the computer, especially if one is available, may well be imprudent.

The last several years has been a period of experimentation with the use of the computer in many areas of undergraduate instruction. In mathematics these have ranged from treating the computer as a "giant slide rule", as is characteristic of use of the computer in many contemporary texts, to the rather profound reorganization of calculus seen in the CRICISAM effort Calculus, a computer oriented approach. The present little book is much less ambitious in scope than the latter of these approaches. However, the author hopes it is closer in spirit to the latter than it is to the former. Certainly, the computer is a giant slide rule but it has been the author's goal to use it and FORTRAN as reason and motivation to develop some mathematical concepts. To assist in achieving the goals, the author has included EXERCISES which appear to be standard calculus problems but for which conventional closed form solutions are not possible, EXERCISES where the exact solutions can be compared with various approximate solutions, and EXERCISES which, from the outset, appear different from those which usually find their way into calculus texts.

Regardless of the approach, most instructors who have used the computer in conjunction with calculus have found the combination fruitful.

Among the benefits which the author has noted in teaching the material in this book for several years are these five:

---

[1] In The Discourses, Chapter XVII.

1) Such combinations show the relative power of both classical calculus and machine methods (for the most part - approximations) in the same context. Each has a role to play and their intermingling seems to make this apparent.

2) While the computer cannot actually carry out "infinite processes", the student using the computer can become much more a participant than a spectator at this sport. It is hoped that this active approach brings students to a deeper understanding of these processes.

3) The algorithmic approach to problem solving, engendered by the computer, seems to focus attention more on the problem to be solved and less on remembering a "formula" with which one "plugs and chugs".

4) The introduction of the idea of an infinite algorithm brings to problem solving and, indeed, to the ideas and processes of calculus an active framework for the contemplation of the ideas of calculus.

5) The student is much more involved with some mathematical concepts and the perception of these sharpened by programming. As an example, the distinction between functions, variables and parameters is often not understood. The FORTRAN concept of an arithmetic statement function provides an excellent vehicle for elaborating both the definitions of and the distinctions between these concepts.

   The author's purpose in writing this book was to emphasize the learning of calculus while learning enough about computing to facilitate the learning of calculus in the ways outlined above. It is recognized that it is not the purpose of courses where this book is used to develop programmers. The organization of material (and exclusions) is influenced by this point of view. However, the FORTRAN material which is included is adequate for most scientific work. Where there is more to learn, it is indicated through footnotes and other references. It is the author's opinion that students who master this text will not require another introductory programming course before embarking on the further study of the computer sciences.

   This book may be used as a companion for almost any calculus text. It may also be used by itself in a companion course of one semester length for students who have completed one or two semesters of calculus. Still another use is in a sequence of mini-courses paralleling the regular calculus sequence. In this application, the instructors of the two courses may even be different persons.

An integration of this book with a typical calculus text is given on page 141. Material is included to augment a course in differential equations. Also included, page 139, is a list of EXERCISES classified by topic.

The only reordering of the material in the typical text is that required by the early introduction of sequences. Sequences are usually introduced late in calculus texts because of their intimate relationship with infinite series. Divorced from series, sequences can be studied at any time. They may even be studied prior to the discussion of the standard concept of the limit of a function because they are basically more intuitive and directly translatable, through the concept of algorithm, into computing techniques which influence our approach to the study of calculus. Indeed, together with the computer and the concept of approximation, they open to study a class of problems which develop an understanding of the fundamental notions of calculus in a way which is impossible in ordinary courses.

The author acknowledges the cooperation of several colleagues who used preliminary versions of this book in their classes. Thanks are due Judy Snider for her excellent typing of the book and James Gleim for his faithful rendition of the author's sketches for the figures.

W.R.F.

West Lafayette, Indiana

1977

Foreword to the student

It was actually a question from a student which led the author to write this book. Picture, if you will, a large lecture room with nearly 400 students in it. Think of the collective effort of these 400 students and their instructor laboring through a rather complicated problem involving applications of the calculus (which you probably haven't yet seen) requiring something like 10 or 15 minutes for its completion. Listen to a student, at the end of this work say/ask: "Professor Fuller, that took x minutes. Don't you know that a computer could handle that in 30 seconds?" Think of the instructor's thoughts as the applause of the 399 other students acknowledged the sagacity of the one!

The instructors thoughts

1) They're wrong - it would only take a computer a few microseconds to solve the problem. It would take hours to prepare it for the machine.

2) They think calculus is obsolete.

3) They don't know the ways in which their perception is wrong.

4) They deserve to know - I'd better plan to tell them.

Here, several years and rewrites later, is the result of that student's question.

It is not, however, merely to correct this misconception that the computer is a valuable adjunct to the calculus course. The judicious use of the computer may actually be an aid in learning some aspects of calculus. Some of the ways it does this are outlined in the Foreword to the Instructor. The use of the computer also helps because it forces the programmer to become a teacher. When you write a program you are "teaching" a computationally fast but witless machine to perform a task. Teaching, or explaining, some subject to another frequently helps our own understanding of the subject. The advantage of teaching a machine is that the teacher reaps the benefit of perfecting his or her technique while the "learner" does not suffer from this period of self-education.

The EXERCISES in this book include some which, it is hoped, are interesting applications of calculus concepts but which, without the computational aid of a machine cannot be attacked and hence are not seen in the traditional calculus course. It will probably be impossible to do all of the EXERCISES. However, computing is learned by doing as is mathematics in general. I hope that you will enjoy the degree of involvement generated by this approach.

W.R.F.

TABLE OF CONTENTS

1. A Little Vocabulary

Communication with the computer involves the preparation of a program which contains, in a form understood by the computer, a set of instructions, data, questions, etc. This program is then either punched in a deck of cards which is mechanically ingested and electrically read by the computer or is typed on a special typewriter known as a Teletype[1]. The computer replies on paper--usually repeating the instructions, data, questions, etc., and then giving its responses, the results of computation. Schematically, this is shown in Figure 1-1.

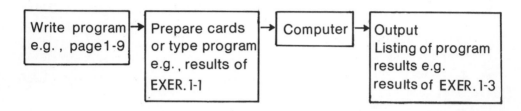

Figure 1-1

Although it has little to do with the operation of the computer from the user's viewpoint, there is a significant jargon about computing. Part of this is important to the beginner as it will help him communicate with other people about his computing problems. In this section many of the terms of this jargon are introduced and defined by the context in which they are found. It is suggested that the reader familiarize himself with these terms.

The data card, Figure 1-2, is ubiquitous. In addition to knowing that one should not be "folded, spindled or mutilated", some nomenclature of the data card is useful. Referring to Figure 1-2, we see that the card contains 80 columns of the digits 0 through 9. We also refer to the zero row, the nine row, etc. Though there is no printed indication of it, computer scientists also distinguish, and use, two other rows - the eleven row, the one above the zero row and the twelve row at the top. Figure 1-2 reveals punches in both these rows. The

---

[1] In this section we shall be concerned primarily with card input. Teletype input varies considerably from installation to installation. Instruction for whatever type of input is to be used will be available from the Computer Center. Teletypes are also known as terminals.

bottom of the card is commonly called the <u>nine edge</u> and the top is
called the <u>twelve edge</u>. The printed side of the card is called the
<u>face</u>. None of this printed material, including that typed by the key-
punch at the top of the card, is of any consequence to the computer.
It reads only the holes.

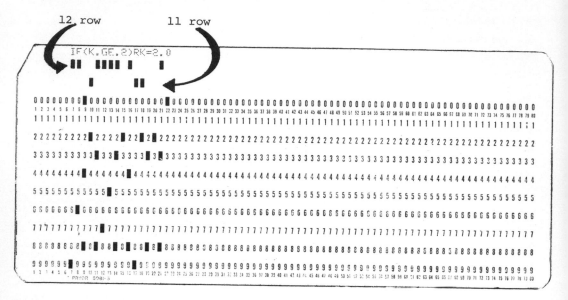

Figure 1-2

We have already indicated that the computer <u>reads</u> cards. It does
this by sensing, electrically, the presence of a hole in a particular
location[1]. The computer is built to respond to the stimuli thus
received in somewhat the same way that an electronic amplifier
responds to the electrical stimuli generated in a microphone. Unfortunately, we cannot yet communicate with a computer orally. Hence,
we must agree on the way the computer is to respond to certain
collections of holes in a card. (Actually, the user rarely partic-
ipates in these agreements. They are made by the manufacturer with
the aim of pleasing as many people as possible.) These agreements
result in what is called a <u>machine language</u>. This is a coded collection of holes which stimulate the computer to perform those
mechanical and electrical operations which correspond, under the code,
to arithmetic operations. Machine languages are usually simple, but
since only the arithmetic operations are allowed, they are extremely

---

[1] In Teletype operation, this electrical indication is generated by
the typewriter.

time consuming to use. In this course we shall not be concerned with
machine language[1]. Languages which are simpler from the user's viewpoint are called <u>problem oriented languages</u>. Among these are FORTRAN
(the language used in this book), COBOL, etc. The instructions to
the computer in one of these languages is called a <u>source program</u>.

Before the computer can use a program written in the FORTRAN
language, or simply "in FORTRAN", the contents must be translated to
machine language. This is done by a special program called a <u>compiler</u>
or a <u>translator</u>. Its operation may be thought of as a simple search
of a dictionary of instructions. The dictionary is entered with a
FORTRAN instruction (or statement) and exitted with a machine
language instruction or set of instructions. As a general rule, each
different computer has supplied with it a unique compiler distinct in
many ways from those supplied with other computers[2]. FORTRAN gets its
name from FORmula TRANslator.

The compiler supplied with a computer is part of what is called
the <u>software package</u>. (To distinguish it from the various material
components of the computer which are called the <u>hardware</u>.) The
supplied software is often supplemented and/or modified by the
operators of a given computer. For example, some computing installations have special versions of FORTRAN for use by beginners. Primarily, these special versions of FORTRAN provide <u>diagnostic</u> statements
to the beginner to indicate the errors which prevented the computer
from carrying out the programmer's intentions. They are very useful
in curing (<u>debugging</u>) sick programs.

There are some limitations on the size of programs and some
reduction in the scope of FORTRAN features under these special systems
but these are of no practical concern here. Furthermore, all the

---

[1]The interested reader may find an introduction to the subject in
<u>Introduction to Computer Science</u> by John K. and John R. Rice; Holt,
Rinehart, Winston, 1969; <u>Introduction to Computers and Problem
Solving</u> by T. E. Hull and D.D.F. Day, Addison Wesley, 1969 or
computer manuals supplied by the manufacturers.

[2]Prior to his first several meetings with a computer, the beginning
programmer has probably thought of "the computer" as an infinitely
complex device with boundless powers to provide answers to questions
put to it by its owners. From an engineering and manufacturing
viewpoint computers are complex (and diverse). The typical user,
however, needs only a superficial view of computers such as given
here. The reader who wishes more information may consult one of the
many elementary books on the subject, such as Rice and Rice,
ibid.

FORTRAN features discussed in the following pages are part of virtually all FORTRAN compilers and, hence, are applicable at most computing installations. In particular the material covered agrees with the USA Standard FORTRAN specifications as published by the United States of America Standards Institute. The Standards Institute also specifies a lower level FORTRAN called Basic FORTRAN. This is not the BASIC language. Deficiencies in USA Standard Basic FORTRAN (SBF) are given in footnotes.

The deck of cards containing the program to be used by the computer is called the source program deck. When it is read by the computer, it is compiled and the corresponding machine language program is called the object program. The source program is returned to the programmer after it has been read and the object program, data and instructions are stored in the computer where it is executed, i.e. the instructions are carried out one after another. An individual who writes source programs is known as a programmer. The operations to be punched (typed) for performance by the computer are given by statements written by the programmer. There are two types of statements: executable and nonexecutable. The former cause computation to take place; the latter cause the computer to interpret statements in various ways. (See, e.g., type statements - Section 2; arithmetic statement functions - Section 4; DIMENSION - Section 9, END, etc.)

The computer is operated by the Computer Center. The equipment of the Center includes the computer itself which is composed of the central processor, which actually performs the high speed computations; the memory unit, where numbers are stored for use by the central processor; and the control unit, which receives, interprets and causes the execution of instructions. Associated with these and also under the control of the control unit are the input/output devices -- tape units, card readers, high speed printers, etc. The Center also provides peripheral equipment such as keypunches (for converting source program statements to source program decks); and tabulators (for listing, i.e., printing on paper, the contents of punched cards) and other items whose use is beyond the requirements of this course. The personnel of the Computer Center includes machine operators, consultants made available by the Center to help find errors in programs, and, at the apex of the system, the systems programmers who design and maintain the complicated programs by which compiling, etc., are operated.

When a program is submitted to the Center for processing, it is called a job. When a job is submitted in the form of a deck, it is physically stored ‧with other jobs until a specified time or number of jobs is reached. All jobs then present are processed serially. This is known as <u>batch</u> processing. The results of computation are called <u>output</u>. The time between submitting jobs and getting back the output is known as the <u>turnaround time</u>. This time becomes a dominant factor in the life of the <u>user</u>, the one who submits jobs. In this course all output will be printed on paper. The output includes a program <u>listing</u>, the numbers which the program asked the machine to generate (assuming the program is correct) and, usually, data from the Computer Center about the time required for execution, etc. Programs which cannot be compiled and run are said to have <u>aborted</u>.

Other items of vocabulary will be introduced from time to time. The presence of new terms will usually be signaled as above by the use of <u>italics</u>. Rarely, will we give formal definitions of terms. The context will usually serve instead.

We conclude this section with some exercises which acquaint the reader with some of the mechanical aspects of computing. These include card punching, listing, submitting a job for batch processing and retrieving the output.

Methods of obtaining the computer's attention and submitting a source program, punched on cards, for processing vary with the installation. Usually, as in Figure 1-3, special cards called <u>control cards</u> introduce your deck and indicate its end. The exact form of the cards will be specified by your instructor or the Computer Center. Following the initial control cards come the cards containing your program. Numerical data, if any, is punched on cards which follow the program deck. There is not much use of data in calculus; its further discussion is deferred to Section 9. Finally, another control card specified by the Center, completes the deck submitted to the computer. An "exploded" view of this deck is given in Figure 1-3. For typewriter

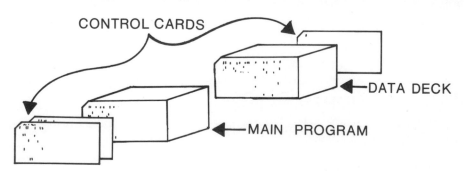

CONTROL CARDS

DATA DECK

MAIN PROGRAM

Figure 1-3

input the form varies only in that instead of being punched in cards, the instructions are typed line by line on paper. Again, the "control lines" will be specified by your instructor or the Computer Center.

A set of typical initial control cards is shown in Figure 1-4. Typically, the final control card is simply a multiply punched card punched with, say, 6/7/8/9 in the first column.

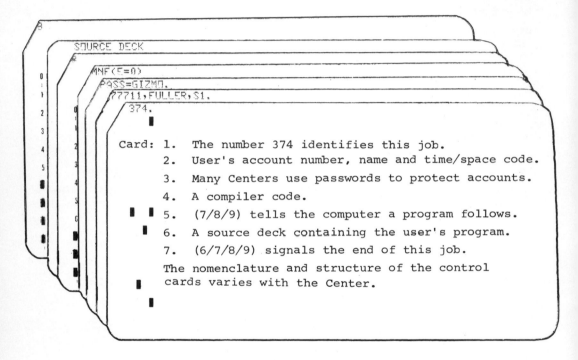

Figure 1-4

Specific details on the form and number of control cards and the physical aspects of job submission will be made available by the Computer Center.

Commencing with the exercises on the next page, you will be submitting your own programs to the computer. To help identify your deck and output, always punch the first card in the source program according to the pattern:

C   PROBLEM X-Y.   YOUR NAME.

EXERCISES

1-1   Obtain from the Computer Center instruction on keypunching or
the use of the terminals. Then, using one card per line,
punch (type) the program in Figure 1-5. It is not necessary
to punch (type) the numbers in columns 79 and 80. These will be
discussed in Section 2. (Do not expect to understand this
program at this time. It is given as an introduction to some
of the mechanics of computing. It will, however, furnish many
examples for new material which will be introduced.)

Punch each and every character in the precise column indicated.
For the first card or line in your program deck punch or type

C   PROGRAM 1-5   YOUR NAME

The symbol Ø is frequently used by programmers to represent
the letter "oh". This avoids inadvertently reading it as "zero".
Other symbols which may be easily confused are the letter I.
the numeral 1 and the symbol / (slant). The reader will
usually recognize which is intended from the context. Human
intelligence makes broad use of context -- artificial intelligence
does not.

1-2   List your deck on the tabulator. See instructions provided by
the Center for using this machine. (Even on a terminal it is
useful to call for a listing before submitting the job for
execution.)

1-3   After satisfying yourself that your program is correctly
punched, submit it for processing. Follow the instructions
provided by the Center concerning control cards and physical
handling of deck. The listing and output of this program are
shown in Figure 1-6. The output may also contain
diagnostic messages concerning errors, or possible errors, and
other data of an accounting nature. This material varies from
Computer Center to Computer Center.

```
C PREFACE THIS PROGRAM WITH APPROPRIATE CONTROL CARDS (FIGURE 1-4).
C THIS PROGRAM APPROXIMATES THE AREA UNDER THE CURVE Y=LOG(F(X)) BETWEEN X=A
C AND X=B TO WITHIN .001 SQUARE UNITS. THE METHOD BOUNDS THE REGION BETWEEN
C INSCRIBED AND CIRCUMSCRIBED RECTANGLES. THE PARTICULAR FUNCTION USED IN
C THIS EXAMPLE IS F(X)=X**2+5. INTL DENOTES THE SUM OF THE INSCRIBED AREAS.
      REAL INTL
      F(X)=X**2+5.
      A=2.
      B=5.
      E=.001
C N IS THE NUMBER OF RECTANGLES USED TO APPROXIMATE THE AREA. WE START WITH 1.
      N=1
C PRINT A HEADING FOR THE OUTPUT TABLE. IN SOME SYSTEMS WRITE(6,1) MUST BE
C USED INSTEAD OF PRINT 1
    1 FORMAT(1X,'WHEN THE NUMBER OF RECTANGLES IS',6X,'THE APPROXIMATION
     1 TO THE AREA IS'//)
C SET UP PARAMETERS TO COMPUTE AREAS OF RECTANGLES. EACH ONE HAS BASE H. K IS
C USED TO COUNT THE RECTANGLES.
    4 K=1
      H=(B-A)/FLOAT(N)
      INTL=0.
      X=A
    2 INTL=INTL+ALOG(F(X))*H
      X=X+H
      K=K+1
C THROUGH LINE 32 THE PROGRAM COMPUTES AND PRINTS THE SUM OF AREAS OF N
C INSCRIBED RECTANGLES.
      IF(K.LT.N)GO TO 2
C THE WRITE MUST BE USED IN SOME SYSTEMS.
   30 C WRITE(6,3)N,INTL
      PRINT 3,N,INTL
    3 FORMAT(14X,I6,30X,F7.3)
C STOP COMPUTING IF THE DIFFERENCE BETWEEN AREAS OF INSCRIBED AND CIRCUM-
C SCRIBED RECTANGLES IS SMALL ENOUGH. (SEE SECTIONS 5 AND 10 FOR REASON.)
      IF(ABS(ALOG(F(B))-ALOG(F(A)))*H.LT.E)STOP
C OTHERWISE DOUBLE THE NUMBER OF RECTANGLES AND REPEAT.
      N=N*2
      GO TO 4
      END
```

Figure 1-5

Listing and Output of Program in Figure 1-5

```
C EXERCISE 1-3.   W.R. FULLER
C PREFACE THIS PROGRAM WITH APPROPRIATE CONTROL CARDS (FIGURE 1-4).
C THIS PROGRAM APPROXIMATES THE AREA UNDER THE CURVE Y=LOG(F(X)) BETWEEN X=A
C AND X=B TO WITHIN .001 SQUARE UNITS. THE METHOD BOUNDS THE REGION BETWEEN
C INSCRIBED AND CIRCUMSCRIBED RECTANGLES. THE PARTICULAR FUNCTION USED IN
C THIS EXAMPLE IS F(X)=X**2+5. INTL DENOTES THE SUM OF THE INSCRIBED AREAS.
      REAL INTL
      F(X)=X**2+5.
      A=2.
      B=5.
      E=.001
C N IS THE NUMBER OF RECTANGLES USED TO APPROXIMATE THE AREA. WE START WITH 1.
      N=1
C PRINT A HEADING FOR THE OUTPUT TABLE. IN SOME SYSTEMS WRITE(6,1) MUST BE
C USED INSTEAD OF PRINT 1
      PRINT 1
    1 FORMAT(1X,'WHEN THE NUMBER OF RECTANGLES IS',6X,'THE APPROXIMATION
     1 TO THE AREA IS'//)
C SET UP PARAMETERS TO COMPUTE AREAS OF RECTANGLES. EACH ONE HAS BASE H. K IS
C USED TO COUNT THE RECTANGLES.
    4 K=1
      H=(B-A)/FLOAT(N)
      INTL=0.
      X=A
C THROUGH LINE 32 THE PROGRAM COMPUTES AND PRINTS THE SUM OF AREAS OF N
C INSCRIBED RECTANGLES.
    2 INTL=INTL+ALOG(F(X))*H
      X=X+H
      K=K+1
      IF(K.LT.N)GO TO 2
C WRITE(6,3)N,INTL MUST BE USED IN SOME SYSTEMS.
      PRINT 3,N,INTL
    3 FORMAT(14X,I6,30X,F7.3)
C STOP COMPUTING IF THE DIFFERENCE BETWEEN AREAS OF INSCRIBED AND CIRCUM-
C SCRIBED RECTANGLES IS SMALL ENOUGH. (SEE SECTIONS 5 AND 10 FOR REASON.)
      IF(ABS(ALOG(F(B))-ALOG(F(A)))*H.LT.E)STOP
C OTHERWISE DOUBLE THE NUMBER OF RECTANGLES AND REPEAT.
      N=N*2
      GO TO 4
      END
```

WHEN THE NUMBER OF RECTANGLES IS	THE APPROXIMATION TO THE AREA IS
1	6.592
2	3.296
4	5.682
8	7.038
16	7.753
32	8.120
64	8.305
128	8.399
256	8.445
512	8.469
1024	8.480
2048	8.486
4096	8.489

Figure 1-6

2. FORTRAN Basics

Writing FORTRAN programs for a computer is like using any other new language. Communication with a native (or a computer) is absolutely necessary, if one is to develop skill and confidence. The reader is urged to develop his linguistic muscles by speaking FORTRAN with a computer on every possible occasion, including, but not restricted to, doing all the computer problems in this book.

In this section we discuss enough of the elements of FORTRAN to allow the reader to commence this "dialogue". Because dialogue includes the ability to obtain a response, later in this section we give simple output instructions which allow the computer to report to us on the results of its computations. We defer complicated output instructions such as on lines 15, 16, 17, 31, 32 of Figure 1-5 until programming mastery has developed.

One of the great advantages of a language like FORTRAN is that the algebraic operations can be written in a form which departs but little from standard notation. The departures are that: multiplication is denoted by an asterisk * and exponentiation by a double asterisk **. Although there are several notations for division in ordinary algebra, only the slant / is used in FORTRAN. Addition and subtraction are denoted in the usual way. Parentheses are the only grouping symbols used in FORTRAN. All of these operations are exemplified in Figure 1-5. On line 7, X**2+5. represents what would ordinarily be written as $x^2 + 5$. One line 21, (B-A)/FLOAT(N) indicates that the difference B-A is to computed first and then the difference divided by the number represented by FLOAT(N). (The explanation of this latter symbol will be given shortly.) On line 37, N*2 indicates that N is to be multiplied by 2. Multiplication and addition are commutative. So N*2=2*N and X+H=H+X. As in algebra, juxtaposition of algebraic operations is illegal. X*-2. must be written -2.*X or X*(-2). In 2.*X, however, X may have a negative value.

In FORTRAN the symbols of arithmetic are executed following the usual hierachy: exponentiation first, then multiplication and division and then addition and subtraction. That is, in an algebraic expression in which there are no grouping symbols (i.e., parentheses) all exponentiations are performed first, then multiplications and divisions (see further on this below) and finally additions and subtractions. Operations enclosed by parentheses are performed independently of the remaining terms in an expression again according to the above rules. Thus, 5.+X**2 cannot be interpreted as (5.+X)**2 and, in Figure 1-5, the expression X**2+5 is distinct from X**(2+5.) and B-A/FLOAT(N) is distinct from (B-A)/FLOAT(N) as usual. When doubt exists as to the need for parentheses, use them. There is no penalty for superfluous parentheses if their pairwise existence would make sense in algebra and would have the desired meaning. E.g., X**2+5. could be written as (X**2)+5. with no change in meaning. Every parenthesis must be paired with a complementary one and the aggregate must convey the meaning intended. For example, Z=(A+B)*C has an altogether different meaning from Z=A+(B*C), just as it does in ordinary algebra. Both, however, make sense and if A,B and C are known in the computer, a value would be assigned to Z in either case. The programmer must be certain that expressions which make sense say what is intended. On the other hand, while a human might compute what was intended from Z=(A+B*C, the FORTRAN compiler will balk at this unbalanced parenthesis and refuse to execute the program in which it appears. In many FORTRAN compilers, the listing of the program in our output would include the <u>diagnostic</u> message "UNBALANCED PARENTHESIS-- EXECUTION DELETED". Such messages help the programmer debug and force him to clarify expressions which would be ambiguous. (A human computer, seeing the one parenthesis above might supply another and compute Z=(A+B)*C when the programmer meant Z=A+B*C and merely left a dangling parenthesis in his program after he realized that the pair in Z=(A+B*C) was not needed.)

Between multiplication and division there is no hierarchical relationship. In most FORTRAN compilers, the operations are performed as encountered in a left to right scan. A/B*C means (A/B)*C not A/(B*C). If A/(B*C) is intended, it must be so written. Again, the use of parentheses to relieve the doubt is always appropriate.

These examples and Figure 1-5 indicate that both variables and constants occur in FORTRAN programs just as they do in algebra. In typical algebra problems, the number of variables rarely exceeds two or three. However, in solving problems on computers, the programmer may well use a dozen or more variables. The programmer often chooses these variable names to be suggestive of the quantity represented. For instance, an expression which will become the numerator of a fraction might be called NUM. If several numerators are involved, they could be enumerated NUM1, NUM2, etc. A variable which records how many of a sequence of operations have been completed might be called COUNT, etc.

Such names are better aids to the memory than more conventional symbols --symbols such as x, y, z, etc.

Considerable latitude exists in FORTRAN in the naming of variables. The only restrictions involve the number and types of characters which may be used and what the first character may be. Names of variables must begin with a letter and may be composed of up to six[1] standard English letters and the digits 0 through 9. (Note: only capital letters may be used.)

Every variable which occurs in a FORTRAN program is assigned a storage location by the compiler. Except for their appearance in "type statements" which will be discussed shortly, "function state-ments" (See Section 4) and certain more esoteric features of FORTRAN, variables will usually occur first on the left side of an equal sign. In any case, before any variable is actually used in a computation it must have a value. This value may be the result of an assignment statement or one the techniques discussed in Section 9. There is, of course, a limit to the total number of variables which can be so stored, but this limit will not be reached by any problem in this book. Further exploration of this question is deferred to courses in programming or computer sciences[2].

A distinctive feature of FORTRAN is that "=" symbolizes <u>assignment</u> to the variable on the left of the value of the right side. Several examples are to be seen by referring to Figure 1-5. On lines 8, 9 and 10 constant values are assigned to the variables A, B and E. Upon encountering these variables, the compiler establishes a storage location for each of them. The statement A=2. causes the constant 2 to be stored in the location assigned (by the compiler) to A. When, for example, A is called for[3] later, as on lines 21, 23 and 35, its value is copied out of this storage location for use. On line 23 the variable X occurs. This causes a storage location to be established for X. The statement X=A found there causes the value stored in A to be copied into X. This does not alter the contents of storage location A. A third type of assignment is given on line 21. Here a storage location is established for H. Into it is read the result of the

---

[1] or five in those compiler which realize only USA Standard Basic FORTRAN (SBF).

[2] Again see Rice and Rice.

[3] Computer scientists use the term "referenced" rather than "called for" The distinction involves a knowledge of compiler/hardware interaction which is beyond the scope of this book.

computation on the right. All of the variables in this computation must, of course, have values stored in the computer. Again, the computation does not affect the stored values of A, B or N.

Another typical, but more surprising, example of an assignment statement is the one on line 27 of Figure 1-5. The meaning of X=X+H is that the values of X and H, which have been previously assigned, are copied from their storage locations and added together to give a new value to X which is then stored in the space set aside for this variable. The value of X which existed before the statement X=X+H was executed will no longer be available. Whenever a variable is referenced, the value used will be the last one, chronologically, which was assigned to that variable by the program. The same thing happens to N at line 37. These meanings are quite different from those attached to such equations in algebra. The statement X = X + H is called _incrementing_ X.

It is sometimes helpful to think of an arrow ← instead of the equal sign. With this notation, the above examples become H←(B-A)/FLOAT(N) and X←X+H. This notation is used in some approaches to teaching FORTRAN but, because it is not available on the standard keypunch, its use has not become widespread.

Statements with other than one variable on the left side of the equal sign cannot be executed in FORTRAN. That is, a statement like X + 4. = 3. has no meaning in FORTRAN even though in ordinary algebra it makes perfectly good sense. This is another minor departure of the FORTRAN language from ordinary algebraic language. It should cause no difficulty once it is accepted.

Lines 8,9,10,12 and 22 assign constant values to A,B,E,N and INTL respectively. Since A,B and E never again appear on the left side of an equal sign, they retain the values initially assigned throughout the program. However, INTL and N have new values assigned on lines 26 and 37. The output obtained from running this program on the computer indicates that these lines are executed many times. How the program accomplishes this, we shall discuss in Sections 3 and 5.

We now discuss some peculiarities in the way FORTRAN compilers view numbers. In simplistic terms, computers recognize two kinds of numbers -- those with decimal points and those without. Those with decimal points are known as _real numbers_ and those without decimal points are known as _integers_. For example, 1. is a real number while 1 is an integer. The computer's arithmetic processes are decidedly different for the two kinds of numbers and in some systems it is not possible to combine a real and an integer (called _mixed mode_) in any algebraic operation except that a real may be raised to an integer power.

Another problem complicating arithmetic on computers is that only numerals with a specified number of digits may be stored[1]. This creates a problem both when dealing with large numbers and when dealing with numbers with many decimal places including very small numbers. Any number which requires more than this number of spaces is "rounded off" in the computer creating an important source of error -- round off error. We deal with these complications in Section 8.

In integer division, FORTRAN offers another novel feature. With the exception of division, all of the arithmetic operations on integers give the expected results, integers. Unexpectedly, division with integers also gives an integer result. When the integer M is divided by the integer N, all the places to the right of the decimal point are dropped. This is an example of truncation. When M/N > 0, the result is [M/N] the greatest integer less than or equal to M/N. When M/N < 0 the effect is slightly more complicated because truncation, in this case, gives a larger rather than a smaller result. Some examples are given in Figure 2-1.

$$4/2 = 2 \qquad\qquad -5/3 = -1$$
$$5/2 = 2 \qquad\qquad -5/(-3) = 1$$
$$-5/2 = -2$$

Figure 2-1

When the remainder, K, in integer division is required, it can be determined from K=M-N*I where I is the integer quotient. Also, if the usual quotient is required it can be obtained by converting the integers to reals as we discuss next.

When one wishes a decimal representation of the ratio of two integers, or a real by an integer, a simple device exists for converting the integers to reals. This device, used on line 21 of Figure 1-5, is the function FLOAT. For any integer, N, the value of FLOAT(N) is a real number of value equal to N. FLOAT is one of several functions supplied in FORTRAN. (See Section 4.)

---

[1]These numbers vary with the computer/compiler. For example, the CDC 6500 FORTRAN compiler allows 15 digits for a real constant and 18 for an integer constant. The IBM 7094 FORTRAN compiler allows 9 digits in a real constant and 11 in an integer constant.

As we have remarked, FORTRAN also allows for the use of variables (symbols which may take on one or more numerical values). Variables are also known as real or integer variables depending on whether the values assigned to them are reals or integers. Except when included in a "type" statment, discussed below, the names of integer variables must begin with one of the letters I,J,K,L,M,N and the names of real variables must begin with one of the remaining letters of the alphabet. IBIS, LIP2, NIL, MINK, L are all examples of integer variables. GRAND, PUNY, RAG2, A, X, Z are examples of real variables.

In many compilers, the above naming conventions can be overridden by a type statement[1]. Such a statement declares the variable(s) in question to be real or integer. MINK is declared to be real by the statement

REAL MINK

while RATE is declared to be an integer by

INTEGER RATE

An example of a type statement is found on line 6 of Figure 1-5 where INTL is declared to be real. Type statements must preceed the first executable statement. Other execution preceding statements will be introduced later and the order among them specified (See Arithmetic statement functions, Section 4; DOUBLE PRECISION, Section 8; DIMENSION, DATA statement, Section 9).

Some programmers do not concern themselves with the naming conventions discussed above. Instead, after they have written a program, they include all variables (even those which follow the conventions) in appropriate type statements. That is, variables which are already real or integer variables may also be declared REAL or INTEGER respectively. Care should be taken not to mix variables of different types in any arithmetic operation.

Except that a real may be raised to an integer power[2] (see X**2+5. in Figure 1-5) reals and integers should not be combined in algebraic operations[3]. None of the mixed mode expressions 1+2.,

---

[1]Type statements are not available in SBF.

[2]When the power is an integer in the usual sense it is preferable to use a FORTRAN integer. E.g., X**2 is preferable to X**2. because the compiler uses a complicated routine involving logarithms on the latter. If the integer power is small it is preferable to avoid exponentiation altogether. I.e., X*X is preferable to X**2, X*X*X is preferable to X**3, etc.

[3]Depending upon the compiler, such combination may or may not be executed at all or may be executed giving erroneous results.

FINAL+6, ICOUNT*1.5, ICOUNT**2.75 is a recommended FORTRAN expression (unless FINAL has been declared an integer and ICOUNT a real in type statements). In most systems, a negative number may not be raised to a real power.

Although reals and integers should not be combined in an arithmetic expression, both types may appear in a single assignment statement. E.g., in a statement such as R=I+L, the sum is computed as an integer but when this value is assigned to R it is stored as a real, since R is real. That is, a change in mode may be effected by an assignment statement. Similarly, in I=X+Y the sum is computed as a real, truncated of its decimal part and stored as an integer. The FORTRAN function analogous to FLOAT for converting reals to integers is IFIX. IFIX truncates as described above. Rounding, as opposed to truncating, X+Y to the nearest integer is accomplished by a statement of the form I=X+Y+.5 when X+Y>0 and I=X+Y-.5 when X+Y<0. IFIX(X+Y+.5) and IFIX(X+Y-.5) give, respectively, the same values. IFIX is useful when one wishes to compute with such values without storing or printing them.

The mode change provided by this use of the assignment statement may be used instead of the functions FLOAT or IFIX if desired. Such a procedure, however, usually requires an extra line in the program. For example, line 21 in Figure 1-5 reads:

    H=(B-A)/FLOAT(N)

This could be replaced by two lines, say[1]:

    RN=N
    H=(B-A)/RN

The following are valid FORTRAN statements:

    MAX=1
    X=P+Q
    R=M+N (The sum of the integers M and N is stored as a real.)
    X=X+H
    I=K/J (Of course, only the integer part is computed and stored.)
    ZED=A+B+C+D**2   (Both Statements compute
    ZED=(((A+B)+C)+D**2)   the same ZED.)

    RUT=PIN/BYE*PIT   (Both Statements are valid but
    RUT=PIN/(BYE*PIT)   compute different values of RUT.)

    Z=(X**2+Y**2)**.5

---

[1] Some compilers allow more than one statement per line. For example, RN=N$H=(B-A)/RN.

The following are invalid FORTRAN statements:

MAX=1+A   (Mixed mode)

ROOT=(1.+(-2.)**1.5)*DEN   (Negative to real power.)

X=3.

Y=1.-X**2

Z=(1.+Y**.5)**2.

(This sequence of steps produces the same type error as in the previous example. If the last exponent were a 2 instead of a 2., this would be valid.)

NEG=X*-2.   (Arithmetic operations juxtaposed. Either -2.*X or X*(-2.) would be valid.)

J=(I**3+2)**.5)   (Integer to real power.)

YMIN==(1.-XMIN**2)**1.5   (Symbol other than letter or digit in variable name, an extra = sign.)

X+3.=FLOAT(N)   (X+3. is not a valid variable name.)

1STMIN=2.*X-3.   (Variable name begins with other than a letter.)

We now discuss a simplified output procedure which will enable us to command the computer to report the results of its labors. We suppose that the values of several variables are stored in the computer. We denote them here as NAME1,NAME2,etc. The values may be either integers or reals, and we must write an appropriate <u>specification</u> in either case. The specifications must be arranged in the same order as the variables.

To print the values of several variables, two statements are needed:

      PRINT k,NAME1,NAME2,...,NAMEn
    k FORMAT(1X,...symbol specifying types of variables...)

where k is a statement number which links the PRINT and FORMAT statements.[1]   k cannot be the number of any other statement.

The symbols specifying variables by type (and size) are:

I15   for each integer variable.

E15.n for each real variable. n specifies the number of decimal places and may not exceed 6. The output has the form $x.y\cdots zE\pm ij$ where $x.y\cdots z$ is a real number and $E\pm ij$ stands for $10^{\pm ij}$. In Section 7 we discuss outputting in standard decimal form as in Figure 1-6.

In this simplified approach, the list NAME1,...,NAMEn can contain no more than 8 variables.

---

[1]PRINT is not required by the Standards Institute for FORTRAN compilers and may not be available at all installations. For the Standards WRITE(n,k) see Section 7.

Suppose the following variables, obeying the naming conventions, are stored in the computer:

S=1.6725   T=0.00000000000013768   I=75

The statements

      PRINT 99,S,I,T
   99 FORMAT(1X,E15.6,I15,E15.6)

would produce the output:

  ~~~0.167250E~01~~~~~~~~~~~~~75~~~0.137680E-12

where ~ represents a blank.

Here the list of variables contains three entries: S, T and I;
two reals and an integer. We have chosen to output them in the order
S, I, T.   Thus, our type specifications are in the same order, namely:
E15.6, I15, E15.6.   The output order T, I, S would not have required
a change in the order of the specifications but the order S, T, I
would require E15.6, E15.6, I15.   We also remark that if p identical
specification occur <u>consecutively</u> that specification need be written
but once, prefixed by a p.   Thus, the last set of specifications could
be written 2E15.6, I15.   The symbol 1X is explained in Section 7.
For now consider it part of the symbol FORMAT.

In this example, the number 99 was chosen for k, the statement
number which links the corresponding PRINT and FORMAT statements. In
Figure 1-5 other examples of such links are found on lines 15 and 16
and on lines 31 and 32.   In Section 7 we discuss these in greater
detail.   The full discussion of these more versatile output commands
is deferred while problem solving power is developing.

Constants may also be input in exponential format.   The form is
rEq, where r is a real number and q is an appropriately signed
integer (exponent) of at most two digits.   Blanks in the exponent may
be omitted.   Thus, 16.892 = 1.6892E1 = .16892E2 = 168.92E-1 =
168920000000.E-10, etc.   As a further example, line 10 in Figure 1-5
could be replaced by: E=1.E-3.   Note that the 1 here is necessary.
E-3 alone would be considered an illegal real variable.

Figure 2-2 show a specially printed card which is useful in
discussing the placement of FORTRAN statements, etc., on cards.
Naturally, none of the printing is of any importance to the computer.
Ordinary data cards (Figure 1-2) may be used for punching source
decks.   References to columns become references to spaces on a line
when using a teletype terminal.

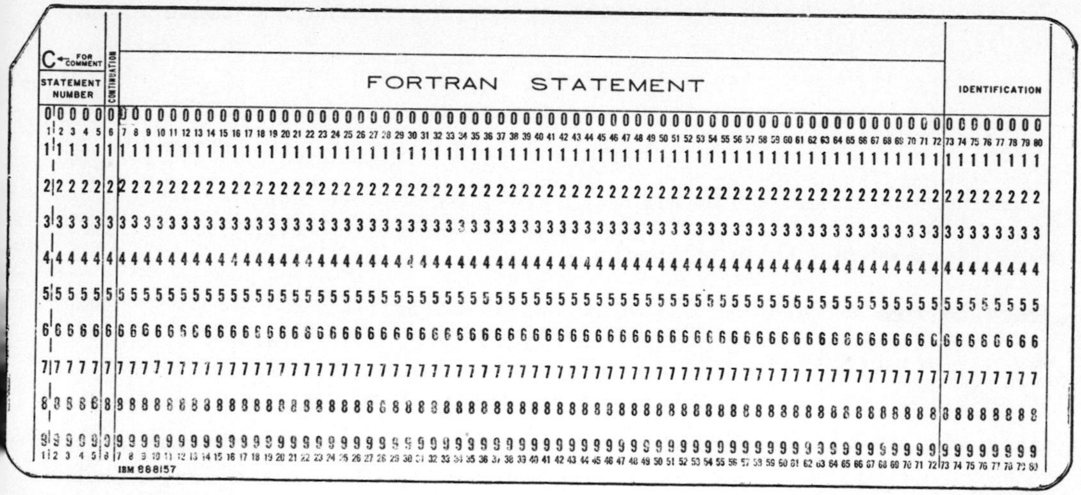

Figure 2-2

An explanation of the terms appearing in Figure 2-2: COMMENT, STATEMENT NUMBER, etc. will now be given.

COMMENT:

If a C is placed in column 1 on any card, the remaining entries on that card are ignored during compilation although the contents of the card are listed along with the rest of the program in the output. This enables the programmer to enter notes in the program which are helpful should another programmer wish to use or modify the program. In fact, they can be helpful to the originating programmer who returns to his program after the passage of considerable time. Figure 1-5 gives several examples of comment cards. Note that all columns 2 through 80 may be used for comments.

STATEMENT NUMBER:

Columns 1-5 are reserved in FORTRAN for statement numbers. Referring again to Figure 1-5 we see that not all statements need be numbered. Those which are numbered there follow an unusual sequence-- 1,4,2,3. On the other hand, all statements may be numbered if the programmer desires it. Statement numbers are necessary when the programmer wishes to transfer control (see Section 3) from one part of the program to another. For example, after the statements on lines 20 through 35 of Figure 1-5 are executed, we encounter the statement N=N*2, that is, an instruction to double N. This is followed by the statement GO TO 4. Although we discuss it in greater detail later, the GO TO statement causes computation to return (in this case) to an earlier point in the program and repeat a sequence of operations. The statement number on line 16 ties the printing of these words to the PRINT statement on line 15, etc. The sequence of statement numbers can be the product of whimsey on the part of the programmer. In Figure 1-5, they follow the order in which their need was discerned by the programmer.

CONTINUATION:

By punching some non-zero character in column 6, the programmer signals the compiler of a FORTRAN statement which is too long for one card. An example is found on lines 16 and 17 of Figure 1-5.

FORTRAN STATEMENTS:

The FORTRAN statements which comprise the program are punched in columns 7-72. Again, see Figure 1-5. On most of the lines, once a statement is begun in column 7, every column up to the last one used contains some symbol. The use of blanks is a matter of convenience, not necessity. Blanks may be inserted as in REAL INT, GO TO 4, etc., in a program or on cards to improve readability (not for the computer). Since inserting these blanks increases typing time, we will usually omit them. Starting a FORTRAN statement in a column to the right of column 7 will cause no trouble. Starting a statement in a column to the left of column 7 will cause the program to abort or produce an erroneous result.

IDENTIFICATION:

Columns 73-80 are ignored by FORTRAN compilers except for listing. They may be used for identification as we have in Figure 1-5. Should the deck become scrambled, these identification numbers may be used to reorder the cards. Their use is entirely optional. They are used in Figure 1-5 only as an illustration. Except in long programs, the added time required to punch these numbers is probably not compensated for by the reordering capability they provide.

END:

The last card in a program source deck must always be END (see line 39 of Figure 1-5). END is a FORTRAN statement. It must be punched columns 7-72.

We have now given several examples of FORTRAN statements and one complete program (Figure 1-5). Since the reader will soon be called upon to write programs, we give some examples which are more than single statements but not yet as complex as Figure 1-5. Many of the features of that program have not yet been discuseed so our first programs will be relatively simple.

Task: Find the area of a triangle if the length of its base 16 3/4 cm. and its altitude is 4 2/7 cm. Output the data and the area.

Analysis: We must program the formula for the area of a triangle or at least the form it takes in this case. We elect the former so that our program will be applicable to other triangles.

Program:

```
C   ENTER CONTROL CARDS AS SPECIFIED BY THE CENTER
C   WE MUST ENTER THE DATA BEFORE WE CAN USE IT.
        H=4.+2./7.
        B=16.+3./4.
        A=H*B/2.
        PRINT 1,B,H,A
      1 FORMAT(1X,3E15.6)
        END
```

Output

~~~1.675000E+01~~~4.285714E+00~~~3.58926E+01

Task: Find the value of $y = x^{16} - x^3 + x^2$ at x = .5, .9, and .999. Plot the three resulting points on a rectangular coordinate system.

Analysis: We are to compute y from the above formula for each of the given values of x. Then we plot each x and its associated y as a coordinate pair.

Program:

```
C   ENTER CONTROL CARDS AS SPECIFIED BY THE CENTER
C   ENTER X VALUES.
        X1=.5
        X2=.9
        X3=.999
C   COMPUTE THE Y VALUES.   (AFTER SECTION 4. WE WILL BE ABLE TO DO THIS
C   MUCH MORE EFFICIENTLY.)   NOTICE THE DIFFERENT EXPONENTIATIONS.
        Y1=X1**16-X1*X1*X1+X1*X1
        Y2=Y2**16-X2*X2*X2+X2*X2
        Y3=X3**16-X3*X3*X3+X3*X3
        PRINT 66,X1,Y1,X2,Y2,X3,Y3
     66 FORMAT(1X,6E15.3)
C   15.3 ALLOWS ENOUGH SPACES TO OUTPUT .999.   USING FEWER WOULD CAUSE
C   X3 TO BE ROUNDED TO 1 ON OUTPUT.
        END
```

PLOT OF THREE POINTS ON THE GRAPH OF $y = x^{16} - x^3 + x^2$

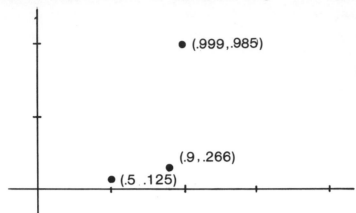

Task: Find the algebraic difference between the result of rounding
to an integer the sum of 63.28, 57.59 and 13.62 and the sum
of the rounded versions of the numbers. Insert a COMMENT card
telling how to determine which is larger.

Analysis: First we are to sum the three numbers and then round this
result. Then we are to round the numbers and sum their rounds.
Finally, we are to compute the difference between these
results and use it to tell which operation gives the larger
number (In this case). We will use the sign of the difference
to supply this information. The only remaining decision is -
what to name the variables. We do this in the program.

Program:

```
C   ENTER CONTROL CARDS AS SPECIFIED BY THE CENTER.
C   WE NAME THE VARIABLES A, B AND C.
      A=63.28
      B=57.59
      C=13.62
C   COMPUTE THE SUM AND ROUND IT.   RECALL NAMING CONVENTION.
      M=IFIX(A+B+C+.5)
C   COMPUTE THE SUM OF ROUNDED NUMBERS.
      N=IFIX(A+.5)+IFIX(B+.5)+IFIX(C+.5)
C   COMPUTE M-N.  IF + THE ROUNDED SUM IS GREATER THAN THE SUM OF THE
C   ROUNDED NUMBERS.  IF - THE ROUNDED SUM IS LESS.  IF 0 THEY ARE EQUAL.
      I=M-N
      PRINT 100,I
  100 FORMAT(1X,I15)
      END
```

Output

~~~~~~~~~~~~~-1

EXERCISES

2-1   Write program segments for each of the following:

(a)   Compute a new value of XNOW by adding .03 to its present value.

(b)   Write an expression which has the value 0 when N, an integer, is even.

(c)   Subtract the sum of the squares of ABSC and ORD from 1.

(d)   Divide SUM by the product of H and 2 in two ways.

(e)   Write a FORMAT statement to accompany PRINT 66, L,B,J which will output the values of the variables L,B.J.

(f)   Assign to SCOR the sum of TEST and INCR.

Answers: (a)   XNOW=XNOW+.03

(b)   N-2*(N/2)   Note: The parentheses are essential.

(c)   1.-(ABSC**2+ORD**2)

(d)   SUM/(H*2.) or SUM/H/2.

(e)   66 FORMAT(1X,I15,E15.6,I15)

(f)   SCOR=TEST+FLOAT(INCR) or, say,

RINCR=INCR
SCOR=TEST+RINCR

2-2   A hexagonal washer 1/2 inch thick is shown in the sketch.   Its density is 0.322 lbs. per cubic inch.   Write and run a program to find the volume and weight of the washer.

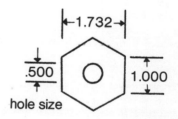

Answer: Vol = 1.200825E+00, wgt = 3.866658E-01
       (Because of our current capabilities our output contains more places than are dictated by the rules of significant figures.)

2-3   A student has test scores of 83, 92, 91, 96 and 92.   Write and run a program to output his average rounded to the nearest integer using both assignment and IFIX.

2-4   Remove the cards punched for lines 15, 16, 17 of Figure 1-5 and
      using the output instructions of this section, write a new line
      for line 32.   Rerun the program using this new FORMAT statement.

2-5   A hollow sphere is made of a metal the density of which is
      19.235 lbs/ft^3.   How much error is made in the weight of a
      sphere whose inside radius is 6 inches if the shell is .018
      inch thick when it should have been .012 inch thick.

Answer: Weight error = 3.036553E-02

3. Branching Statements

Many problems of calculus involve asking if a specified operation has been done enough times, whether or not a certain function is small enough, or whether or not two approximations to a certain quantity are near enough in value to each other. If the answer to one of these is YES, we may wish a program to proceed in one way; if the answer is NO, in another. The FORTRAN features which provide this capability are the logical IF[1] and the GO TO statements.

One typical use of GO TO is found on line 38 of Figure 1-5. There, after a sequence of steps culminating in the doubling of N, we find the statement GO TO 4. This causes computation to transfer immediately to statement number 4 on line 20 following which the computer again processes the statements beginning with 4. When lines 20 through 37 are executed this time (i.e., on this pass) N and, hence H, has a different value from the one on the previous pass. In a statement such as GO TO k, k must be the number of an executable statement. The only non-executable statements which we have encountered thus far are type statements, FORMAT and END.

The use of the logical IF in conjunction with a GO TO provides the branching described in the first paragraph. The form is:

    IF(A relation B)GO TO k
    NEXT STATEMENT

where A and B are FORTRAN expressions computable in terms of data stored in the computer. The GO TO is executed if A is in the indicated relation to B and NEXT STATEMENT is executed if it is not. The logical IF is used in this way on line 29 of Figure 1-5. (The symbol .LT. means "less than". We discuss other such symbols in a moment.) A similar use of the logical IF is made on line 35 where the affirmative branch terminates the program with the FORTRAN statement STOP. We shall have another word to say about STOP later in this section.

In Figure 1-5, K is used to count the rectangles used in approximating the area. On line 29 we ask if K < N? If it is, we must continue to add areas of rectangles to INTL. (We could also use,

---

[1]Not available in SBF. The Arithmetic IF (Section 9) must be used.

on line 29, IF(X.LT.B) GO TO 2 but because of roundoff error this is less reliable than actually counting the rectangles.) When an affirmative answer is received, GO TO 2 is executed and computation returns to line 26. If X ⩾ B, we do not wish to execute line 26 again. (The reason for this is discussed more fully in Section 10. It is due to having computed the areas of all non-overlapping rectangles of base H which can be inscribed between the x-axis and the graph of y=log(x^2+5) on the interval [2,5].) Instead, we print the value of N and INTL then stored in the computer. The computer then executes consecutively lines 31 and 32 and comes to line 33.

As we have remarked, if on line 35 of Figure 1-5, h·|log(f(b))-log(f(a)| < .001 the STOP statement is executed and the program terminates. (The reason for the criterion involved in stopping will be clear after Section 5 is studied.) Otherwise, NEXT STATEMENT, which in this case doubles N, is executed and the statement GO TO 4 causes all the computations on lines 20 through 32, at least, to be repeated. This answers the question as to how N and INTL are assigned new values repeatedly.

The existence and desirability of alternate stopping mechanisms is discussed in Exercise 3-3 (b) at the end of this section.

A block of statements which is executed repeatedly such as on lines 26 through 29 of Figure 1-5 is called a loop. Such loops are characteristic of most computing problems. Lines 20 through 38 also form a loop. Since this loop contains another loop, the combination is sometimes referred to as a nest of loops.

The power of the logical IF comes from the large number of logical relations and connectives which can be used with it. We have already seen .LT. used in Figure 1-5. The full set of relations is:

Relation	Algebraic equivalent
.GT.	greater than
.LT.	less than
.EQ.	equal
.NE.	different from
.LE.	less than or equal
.GE.	greater than or equal

A second use of the logical IF is as follows:

```
IF(A relation B)STATEMENT 1
STATEMENT 2
```

Here, we suppose that STATEMENT 1 is neither a GO TO nor a STOP.   In
this case, if A is in the indicated relation to B, STATEMENT 1 is
executed <u>and</u> <u>then</u>, since there has been no transfer of control to
another part of the program, STATEMENT 2 is executed.   This use of
the logical IF does not appear in Figure 1-5 so we give an example:

Task: Write a program which assigns values to I and J and which sets
       ISIGN=1 if I divides J and otherwise sets ISIGN=-1.   Print I,
       J and ISIGN.

Program:

```
    I=
    J=
    ISIGN=-1
    IF(J.EQ.I*(J/I))ISIGN=1
    PRINT 1,I,J,ISIGN
  1 FORMAT (1X,3I15)
    END
```

Note that we first set ISIGN=-1, the "otherwise", and then change
it only if I does divide J.   The statement ISIGN=1 is executed only
when I divides J.   However, whether or not ISIGN=1 is executed control
passes next to the PRINT statement which plays the role of STATEMENT 2
in this example.

IFs can also be cascaded.   That is, several can appear, one after
another.

Task: Write a program which sets ISIGN=0 if J=5, sets ISIGN=1 if J
       is divisible by both 3 and 7 and otherwise sets ISIGN=-1.

Program:

```
    ISIGN=-1
    IF(J.EQ.5)ISIGN=0
    IF(J.EQ.(3*7)*(J/(3*7)))ISIGN=1
    PRINT 1,J,ISIGN
  1 FORMAT(1X,2 I15)
    END
```

Except for such transfer of control statements as the GO TO and
STOP studied in this section, source programs are executed line by
line in the order written by the programmer.

The logical connectives are .AND. and .OR..   With them compound
logical expressions can be programmed.   For example, if control is to
be transferred to statement 10 if A≥B <u>and</u> C≥D, and to statement 11
otherwise;   we could write:

```
    IF(A.GE.B.AND.C.GE.D)GO TO 10
    GO TO 11
```

If control is to be transferred to 10 if either A≥B or C≥D (or both) we could write:

```
    IF(A.GE.B.OR.C.GE.D)GO TO 10
    GO TO 11
```

It is not necessary for the beginning programmer to spend much time with the connectives, for the same effects can be achieved without them. For instance, the above two examples can be rewritten:

```
    IF(A.GE.B)GO TO 100
    GO TO 11
100 IF(C.GE.D)GO TO 10
    GO TO 11
```

and

```
    IF(A.GE.B)GO TO 10
    IF(C.GE.B)GO TO 10
    GO TO 11
```

respectively.

It may be instructive to follow through at least the first of these alternative examples. Since A≥B and C≥D must both be satisfied, A<B would alone indicate a negative response and control could be transferred to the statement numbered 11 without checking C≥D. If A≥B, then C≥D must be checked. GO TO 100 causes this to be done next. Both A≥B and C≥D must be verified before the program moves to statement 10. If either fails to be true, the program branches to statement 11. The reader should verify the second alternative.

An interesting application of the logical IF is given below. Suppose it is desired to run a program for each of M values of a parameter A. Suppose that the values of the parameter are such that they cannot be obtained one from another by simple incrementation. We proceed as follows:

```
    K=1
100 IF(K.EQ.1)A=X1
    IF(K.EQ.2)A=X2
    IF(K.EQ.3)A=X3
    IF(K.EQ.4)A=X4
       .
       .
       .
    IF(K.EQ.M)A=XM
       .
       .
       .
    MAIN PROGRAM
       .
       .
       .
    IF(K.EQ.M)STOP
    K=K+1
    GO TO 100
    END
```

In Section 9 we discuss an easier method to accomplish this using a data deck.

The promised additional remarks on STOP conclude this section. As we have remarked, STOP causes computing to terminate. There can be several STOP statements in a program if there are several stopping criteria, the satisfaction of any one of which is sufficient. On the other hand, no STOP statement is required. Some programs such as the examples starting on page 3-27 simply terminate with the END statement. The last example may also be written without a STOP statement. Doing so is left as an exercise for the reader.

Equality of reals should not be used as a stopping (or branching) criterion. This is because most reals do not have exact representations in the computer and accumulations of their rounded representations may fail to produce an expected result. We comment further on rounding problems in Section 8.

Again we remark that every program must have an END statement card which is always the last card, physcially, in the source program deck.

Further examples of the logical IF:

Task: $y = 2x - 1$ if $-3 \le x \le 1$ but $y = x^2$ if $x > 1$.
Write a program to compute and print the values of x and y for $-3 \le x \le 3$ at intervals of 0.1.

Program:

```
      X=-3
    2 IF(X.LE.1.)Y=2.*X-1.
      IF(X.GT.1.)Y=X*X
      PRINT 1,X,Y
    1 FORMAT(1X,2E15.6)
      IF(X.GE.3.)STOP
      X=X+.1
      GO TO 2
      END
```

We call attention to several features of this program. Note that we need not ask if x>-3. We simply start at x=-3. Because not both x<1 and x>1 can be true, only one value of y is associated with any one value of x by the IFs on lines 2 and 3. After printing the pair x,y, we ask if x≥3. We really wish to stop with x=3. However, since x is the result of computation its value in the computer may not be exact. (The value output by the procedure given in Section 2 will produce an x rounded to its correct value.)

```
      IF(X.EQ.3.)STOP
```

might never be satisfied causing the computer to continue to compute pairs x,y until some time limit built into the system forced its termination. If we pass the STOP, x is incremented by 0.1 and computation is returned to statement 2 where computation of another x,y pair is started.

Compare the following program with the one just studied.

Program:

```
    X=-3.
  2 Y=2.*X-1.
    IF(X.GT.1.)Y=X*X
    PRINT 1,X,Y
  1 FORMAT(1X,2E15.6)
    IF(X.GE.3.)STOP
    X=X+.1
    GO TO 2
    END
```

There is often more than one program which performs a given task.

A better method of terminating computation in these programs would be to count the number of incrementations of x. This is left as an exercise for the reader.

EXERCISES

3-1   In this problem you are writing a portion of a program. Assume that any variables called for have values of the indicated type stored in the computer.

(a)   If K is greater than COUNT, execute statement 100 next; otherwise, execute 101.

(b)   If X is strictly between 2 and 4, set K=K+1 and then execute statement 7 but, if X is not strictly between 2 and 4, merely execute statement 7. (Note: also try .OR. instead of .AND.)

(c)   If the coordinates (x,y) of a point are inside the unit circle, print them and execute statement 37; otherwise, halve them and execute statement 76.

(d)   If I is odd (recall integer division in Section 2), increase SUM by twice F(X); otherwise, increase SUM by four times F(X). Then, increment I by 1. (The meaning of F(X) will be discussed in Section 4.)

(e) If $F(B) \cdot F(C) < 0$, set $A = C$;   if $F(A) \cdot F(C) < 0$, set $B = C$
     and execute statement 20 next.   If neither, Print C and stop.

(f) Increment X by one one-hundredth of the length of the
     interval $[A,B]$.   If $A \leq X < B$, set $Y = F(X)$ and execute
     statement 3;   otherwise, stop.

Answers:

(b)   IF (X.GT.2..AND.X.LT.4.)K=K+1
        7 .....

(d)   SUM=SUM+2.*F (X)
          IF (I.EQ.2* (I/2)) SUM=SUM+2.*F (X)
          I=I+1

(f)   X=X+ (B-A)/100.
          IF (X.LT.A.OR.X.GE.B) STOP
          Y=F (X)
          GO TO 3

3-2   Square roots occur frequently in physical and geometrical
       problems.   Several methods exist for finding the square root of
       A to any desired degree of accuracy (not all equally suited to
       machine computation).   Here are two:

       (i)   Averaging method: XNEW=.5(XOLD+A/XOLD) is nearer $\sqrt{A}$ than
             XOLD.   Repeat, replacing XOLD by XNEW, until $XNEW^2-A$ is
             sufficiently small.

       (ii) Sum of odd numbers: (I.e., $1 + 3 + 5...+ 2n - 1 = n^2$)
             (To apply to decimals, first multiply by 10^{2k} for the
             smallest k which will clear the fractional part.   Divide
             result by 10^k.)

       (a)   Show that $XNEW^2-A \geq 0$

       (b)   By mathematical induction, prove the formula in (ii) for
             positive integers.

3-3   (a)   Write and run a program to use (i) to compute an
             approximation to $X = \sqrt{16.23}$ so that X^2 differs from 16.23
             by less than .001.

Answer: 4.028648E+00

(b) Modify the above program to count the number of approximations (iterants) required to reach the specified accuracy. Also include a provision for stopping if the required accuracy is not achieved in 15 approximations. When the required accuracy is achieved, output A, N and the approximation to $\sqrt{A}$. Otherwise merely output A and N. Such alternate stopping mechanisms should usually be inserted in programs which otherwise might be unduly expensive of machine time.

3-4 Write and run a program to use (ii) to compute an approximation to $\sqrt{16.23}$, $\sqrt{4.3256}$, $\sqrt{53.46091}$ correct to 3 decimal places.

Answer: $\sqrt{53.46091}$ = 7.312000E+00

3-5 Rewrite one of the programs on Page 3-29 or 3-30 so that the number of incrementations of x is used as the criterion for stopping. Run both your program and the one in the text.

4.   Supplied Functions.   Statement Functions.

     With this section we conclude the study of all the FORTRAN
statements necessary to perform calculations like those programmed in
Figure 1-5.   (We still have not studied output statements such as on
lines 15,16,17,31 and 32.   But the simplified output instructions at
the end of Section 2 enable us to output the essential results.)   Here
we discuss two ways in which functions occur in FORTRAN programs.   In
the first, the programmer uses a function whose definition is supplied
as part of the software.   FLOAT and IFIX (Section 2) are examples of
such supplied functions.   We discuss others below.   In the second, the
programmer writes a definition of the function into his program as on
line 7 of Figure 1-5.

     Most readers have encountered the concept of function at some
time.   Various definitions are given.   Representative ones are:

A.   A function, f, is a correspondence between two sets, D and R,
     of numbers, such that to each element of D there corresponds
     one and only one element of R and every element of R corresponds
     to at least one element of D.   Notationally, if $x \in D$ and $y \in R$
     corresponds to x, we write $y = f(x)$.

B.   A function, f, is a set of ordered pairs such that no pairs
     having distinct second elements have the same first element.
     Notationally, if x is a first element, we write the pair as
     $(x, f(x))$.

     Here we prefer the first typical form because it is a more active
description of the concept and because it more nearly corresponds to
the "assignment" concept which we discussed in Section 2.

     Several familiar functions will no doubt occur to the reader.
These include the trigonometric functions and their inverses, and
probably the exponential and logarithmic functions.   From the fact
that values of these functions are given in tables and only at certain
intervals in their domains, the reader has probably concluded that
constructing values of these functions is not as easy as constructing
those of a polynomial.   This conclusion is correct.   Fortunately, the
software package supplied with the computer contains programs for
calculating the values of all the functions referred to above and more.
These functions are called supplied functions to distinguish them from

those the programmer himself writes. The theory of such calculations
is part of the study of infinite series considered later in your
calculus text. (See also Section 11 of this book.)

Table 4-1 lists supplied functions which are usually available
and which are of the greatest utility in calculus. Note that all
functions names obey the naming conventions discussed in Section 2.

TABLE 4-1

Name	Usual Notation	FORTRAN Symbol	Argument Type	Value Type
Exponential[1]	e^x	EXP(X)	Real	Real
Common logarithm[2]	log x	ALOG10(X)	Real (positive)	Real
Natural logarithm	ln x	ALOG(X)	Real (positive)	Real
Sine	sin x	SIN(X)	Real[3]	Real
Cosine	cos x	COS(X)	Real[3]	Real
Square root	$\sqrt{x}$	SQRT(X)	Real (positive)	Real
Absolute value	$\lvert x \rvert$ $\lvert n \rvert$	ABS(X) IABS(N)	Real Integer	Real Integer
Arctangent	arctan x	ATAN(X)	Real	Real[3]
Convert to real		FLOAT(N)	Integer	Real
Convert to integer (by truncation)		IFIX(X)	Real	Integer

Supplied functions, evaluated at any variable of appropriate
type with stored value, may be called for at any point of a program
just as a variable or constant may. For example, on line 21 of
Figure 1-5 the function FLOAT evaluated at the existing value of N
is used as the value FLOAT(N). This is, of course, the meaning of
FLOAT(N) in mathematics. A supplied function may _never_ appear on the
left side of an equal (=) sign. That is, a supplied function can
never have a value assigned to it in an assignment statement.

---

[1] e=2.71828...is an important constant. It is the base of the natural
logarithm.

[2] The common logarithm is not part of SBF.

[3] In radian measure.

When a supplied function is employed in a program, its argument may also be any valid FORTRAN expression. For example, if XPHAS and PI are stored in the computer, the statement

    Y=3.*COS(PI/2.+XPHAS)

is legitimate and causes the expected value to be stored in location Y ready for further use. As remarked when discussing assignment statements in Section 2, this process leaves the contents of PI and XPHAS unchanged. Supplied functions may also be composed, as in mathematics, the value of one function serving as the argument for another. An example is

    ZED=ALOG(ABS(COS(PI/4.)))

which assigns the expected value to ZED. As usual the range of the inner function must be compatible with the domain of the outer function.

In addition to these supplied functions which are generally available, many computing installations maintain a library of special purpose functions which can be called for in programs in the same way as supplied functions. We shall say another word on this in Section 9 where we discuss subroutines and subprograms.

Using the concept of the statement function, the programmer may also write functions of his own. These functions may then be called for, in the program in which they are defined, in the same way as supplied functions. The statement function has the form

    NAME(ARG1,ARG2,...,ARGN)=EXPRESSION

where NAME (which could be just F if desired) is the name of the function and EXPRESSION is a valid FORTRAN expression involving the dummy variables ARG1,ARG2,...,ARGN plus (a) constants, (b) other variables (with values established before execution of NAME is called for), (c) supplied and library functions and (d) previously defined (in the same program) statement functions. The usual naming conventions must be observed. NAME should not be the name of a supplied function. In some compilers such usage may cause the program to abort. At the very least the supplied function cannot be used elsewhere in the same program.

Statement functions must precede all executable statements. They follow type statements. As noted above, any statement function which refers to another statement function must follow that function. Statement functions can be composed with each other, with supplied functions and vice versa.

Examples of some of these concepts are found in Figure 1-5. On line 7 a statement function is defined. The name of this function is F. The dummy variable used as ARG in defining the function is X. The FORTRAN expression defining the function is given on the right side of the equal sign. Any other legal FORTRAN variable could have been used in place of X on both sides of the equal sign. For example

F(ABSC)=ABSC**2+5.

could have been used since the variable in the definition is merely a dummy, telling the compiler how the value of the function is to be constructed when called for. This, of course, is not different from the usual mathematical meaning of such symbols. The value of the statement function F is employed on line 26 as F(X) and on line 35 as F(A) and F(B). The statement function F is also composed with the supplied function ALOG in both these instances. Since F only occurs in Figure 1-5 composed with ALOG, it could have been defined this way. That is, F could have been defined as

F(X)=ALOG(X**2+5.)

Naturally, some other changes in the program would have resulted from this form of the definition.

Function definitions may also involve parameters. The difference between parameters and variables is in their use. For example, y = mx, in FORTRAN

Y(X) = M*X,

is frequently referred to as a one-parameter family of functions. The functional relationship is between x and y but m is clearly involved in determining the relationship. When m is given then y(1),y(-3), etc., all have well defined meanings both to humans and machines. Without a stated meaning for m y(1), y(-3), etc., are meaningless, at least to a computer. In practice, m is specified first and then y = mx is studied, used, etc., for all x in some domain.

The distinction between variables and parameters in a FORTRAN function can be stated succinctly. If a (legal) symbol appears as one of the arguments of NAME on the left side of the defining expression it is a variable. If it appears only in EXPRESSION it is a parameter. For example, in

Y(X) = M*X

M is a parameter and X is a variable. Further, in

F1(R) = EXP(-R)*PAR*SIN(R)

PAR is a parameter and R is a variable. On the other hand, in

        FN(R,PAR) = EXP(-R)*PAR*SIN(R)

both R and PAR are variables.

  The dummy variables in a statement function may also be replaced by legal FORTRAN expressions. Thus,

        VAL=FN(X+3.*DEX,PAR0+TNCR)

assigns to VAL the same value as the three steps

        X=X+3.*DEX
        PAR=PAR0+TNCR
        VAL=FN(X,PAR)

or, for that matter, something like

        XNEW=X+3.*DEX
        SCALE=PARO+TNCR
        VAL=FN(XNEW,SCALE)

  In all of these examples, the use of symbols in FORTRAN is identical with their use in mathematics. The arguments in a statement function need not be all of the same type. Their use, however, must obey the usual rules for mixing types.

  The distinction between these uses of symbols may be sharpened by considering the following two examples which compute the same value of QUE.(T and S must be known in the computer. FN and Fl are as defined above.)

        QUE=6.*FN(SIN(2.*S)+3.*COS(T),SQRT(S**2+T**2))

and

        PAR=SQRT(S**2+T**2)
        QUE=6.*Fl(SIN(2.*S)+3.*COS(T))

  Finally, we offer an example of a statement function referencing another statement function:

        G(X) = X**2*EXP(-X)
        F(X) = G(X)*4.*COS(X+PHI)

Here F(X) refers to the previously defined statement function G, the supplied function COS, the constant 4. and the variable PHI. Reversing the order of F and G would prevent execution of the program if F was actually called for.

  A function which accurs only once in a program need not be introduced as a statement function. However, when it occurs several times, as F does in Figure 1-5, the statement function procedure reduces both keypunch (typing) time and opportunity for error.

Except for output formatting, we can now perform all of the computations exemplified in Figure 1-5.

EXERCISES

4-1   Write an arithmetic statement function for:

    (a)   the ordinate of $Bx^2\sin x$ as a function of the abscissa.

    (b)   the smaller root of $ax^2 + bx + c$, $a > 0$, as a function of a,b and c.

Answer:

  (a)   ORD(X)=B*X**2*SIN(X)

  (b)   ROOT(X)=(-B-SQRT(B**2-4.*A*C)/(2.*A)

4-2   Find all the angles of a triangle if its sides are a=2.435, b=3.012 and c=2.103. (Suggestion: use the law of cosines to get, say, cos α. Express sin α in terms of cos α and hence compute tan α; then use the supplied arctangent function to get α.)

4-3   Let $f(x) = \sqrt{1+\cos x}$ for $0 \le x \le 4\pi$ and $g(x) = x + (\sqrt{2}-4\pi)$ for $4\pi \le x \le 20$. Compute, in increments of x=.5, and print the coordinates (x,y) of a curve which is the union of {graph of f on its domain} and {graph of g on its domain}. (π=3.14159)

Answer check points: (0,1.414214E+00), (9.000000E+00,2.981103E-01), (1.100000E+01,1.002210E+00), (1.300000E+01,1.847854E+00).

4-4   Let $y = z + 2$ for $z < -1$, $y = 1$ for $-1 \le z \le 0$ and $y = z^2 + 1$ for $z > 0$. Also, let $z = 2 \sin 2x$. Compute y as a function of x for $0 \le x \le 2\pi$ at intervals of .2. Print the pairs (x,y) thus determined.

5.   Algorithms and Flow Charts

Before proceeding, the reader is asked to write out a description of what the program in Figure 1-5 does.

Your description may have varied from the rather general description given on the COMMENT card in that program to a verbatim English translation of the successive lines in the program.   An adequate, but minimal description of a problem of this type would be "To approximate the area between a curve[1] and the x-axis on the interval [a,b], divide the interval into several equal parts.   At the end point of each of these subintervals, compute the length of the ordinate to the curve.   Add together the areas of the rectangles having these ordinates as altitudes and one of the equal subintervals of [a,b] as base.   Check to see if the difference between the sum of the areas of the circumscribed rectangles (see Figure 5-1) and the inscribed rectangles (see Figure 5-2) is smaller than 0.001.   If it is, stop computing and record the sum of the areas of the inscribed rectangles.   If it is not, double the number of rectangles and repeat all of the above."

With the above instructions a reasonably intelligent person could, with the help of a table of logarithms, compute "the approximate area" indicated.   A set of such "step-by-step" instructions for solving a

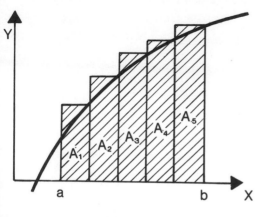

Figure 5-1

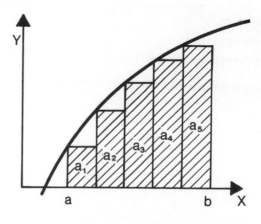

Figure 5-2

problem or performing any task, is called an _algorithm_. A set of instructions for baking a cake or assembling a record rack is thus an algorithm.

Some algorithms, like the minimal description of Figure 1-5 given above, leave some instructions for the reader to supply: such as how many subintervals of [a,b] should be used initially, the preliminary work to reduce the comparison of the two areas in our minimal description to the first expression in the IF on line 35 (the reader should verify this reduction), or the method used on lines 20-29 to accumulate the sum of the areas of the inscribed rectangles without requiring the intermediate storage of, possibly, thousands of numbers representing the areas of these rectangles.

Some algorithms are very detailed. For example, an old recipe for rabbit stew starts--"Catch a rabbit and..." As can be imagined, algorithms which are to become instructions to a computer must be completely detailed. No choices can be left to the machine. For example, it might be left to a human computer to choose the initial value of N (line 12) in Figure 1-5. In most systems all unspecified variables are initialized to 0 or 0.. Since doubling N is an essential feature of Figure 1-5, the choice of initial value of N clearly cannot be left to the computer. In some systems all variables must be initialized. In one of these, an unspecified variable in a program might earn the programmer a diagnostic statement similar to:

"UNIDENTIFIED ARGUMENT ENCOUNTERED AT LINE 21. EXECUTION DELETED."

Similar statements would appear in the programmer's output at each instance where N is called for. It is probably obvious that, at several other points in the program, steps are taken which require detailed advance planning.

Before taking up some ideas to be used in planning programs, we offer two more examples of simple tasks together with the detailed instructions necessary if a computer is to carry out the tasks.

(a) Task: Compute and print the first twenty positive integral powers of 2.

Program:

```
    N=1
  2 Y=2.**N
    PRINT 3,N,Y
  3 FORMAT(1X,I15,E15.0)
    IF(N.EQ.20)STOP
    N=N+1
    GO TO 2
    END
```

(b) Task: Compute the value of $\displaystyle\sum_{N=1}^{K}\frac{1}{1+N^2}$ for K=1,2,3,...,20.

Program: (Compare the straight forward solution at the left with the refined one at the right.)

```
        RK=1.                          F(X)=1./(1.+X*X)
     3  RN=1.                          RK=1.
        SUM=0                          SUM=1./2
     2  SUM=SUM+1./(1.+RN*RN)       2  PRINT 1,RK,SUM
        IF(RN.GE.RK)GO TO1          1  FORMAT(1X,E15.2,E15.6)
        RN=RN+1.                       IF(RK.GE.20.)STOP
        GO TO 2                        RK=RK+1.
     1  PRINT 5,RK,SUM                 SUM=SUM+F(RK)
     5  FORMAT(1X,E15.2,E15.6)         GO TO 2
        IF(RK.GE.20)STOP               END
        RK=RK+1.
        GO TO 3
        END
```

Although neither of the above tasks is difficult in itself, the planning which was necessary to write the programs probably goes far beyond that usually done by the average reader before starting a similar exercise. The question is: "How does one plan a program which will provide complete instructions to a computer to perform computations which the human mind would sequence tacitly?" That is, how does one write a computing algorithm which is completely detailed, yet of practical utility? The answer is provided by the concept of a flowchart. [1]

A flowchart is a schematic diagram of the successive steps in an algorithm for solving a problem which the programmer wishes to have undertaken by the computer. As with all schematic approaches, it is necessary to describe the set of elements from which flowcharts will be built. An examination of the problems undertaken to date indicates that programs are made up of assignments, interrogations, stops, directions to move to another step in the program and print. Some programmers also like to distinguish between those elements of a program which are of an intrinsic nature from those that may be varied from problem to problem. For example, lines 7 through 10 in Figure 1-5 may be varied to provide a whole class of problems solvable by the same program. The reader will doubtless be able to apply it to an even wider class by defining f(x) = ln(x² + 5) and making other appropriate changes in the program. We shall use the symbols in Table 5-1 to represent these elements of a program.

_____

[1] The reader is also referred to the subject of structured programming.

TABLE 5-1

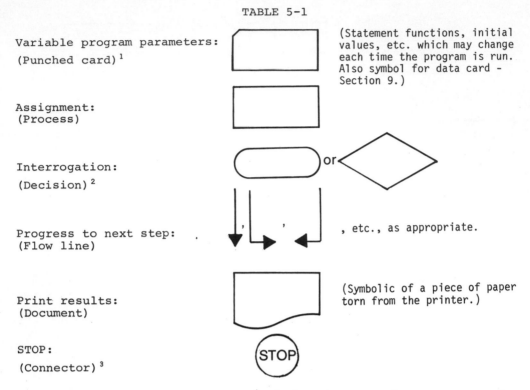

Variable program parameters:
(Punched card)[1]

(Statement functions, initial values, etc. which may change each time the program is run. Also symbol for data card - Section 9.)

Assignment:
(Process)

Interrogation:
(Decision)[2]

or

Progress to next step:
(Flow line)

, etc., as appropriate.

Print results:
(Document)

(Symbolic of a piece of paper torn from the printer.)

STOP:
(Connector)[3]

STOP

Before constructing some actual flowcharts, a few more comments are appropriate. In general, more than one assignment may be made per assignment box. Those to which the program is to return are usually kept separate from those which are fixed once for all or used only initially. (The initialized values of variables.) The interrogation symbolizes the logical IF and, hence, represents a branch in the program. Schematically this would appear:

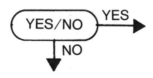

YES/NO YES

NO

Flowcharts for the programs of Tasks (a) and (b) of the above example are given in Figure 5-3 and Figure 5-4 respectively.

[1] The names in parentheses are those preferred by the American Standards Institute.

[2] The second symbol is preferred by ASI. Because long expression cause the diamond to have excessive altitude, the School Mathematics Study Group (SMSG) symbol is used in this book.

[3] In ASI usage the circle is also used to connect portions of a lengthy flowchart.

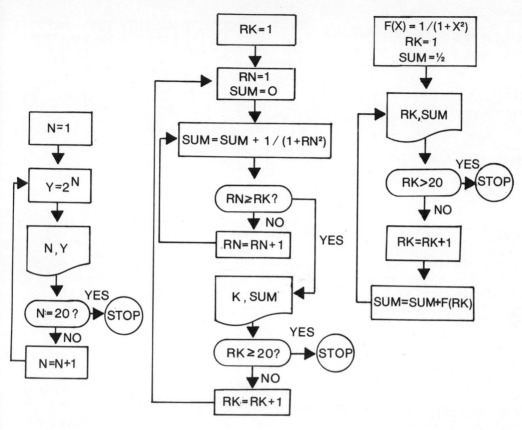

Figure 5-3   Figure 5-4

Note that in these flowcharts we have made no effort to restrict ourselves to the notations, modes, etc., of FORTRAN. These are necessary only in the actual source programs submitted to the computer.

In Figure 5-5 we present a flowchart of Figure 1-5, modified so that the class of functions to which it is applicable is wider than those of the form $\ln(f(x))$.

Naturally, one does not usually start with a program and derive its flowchart. Hence, we next consider the problem of constructing a flowchart directly from the statement of a problem and then write a program from the flowchart. For this purpose let us digress a bit from calculus and find all of the "perfect" numbers less than or equal to one thousand.

Set initial quantities.

Compute length of base of
one rectangle.

Start at left end point with
"area"=0.

Add to the "area" the area of
the rectangle which has the
current value of X as left end-
point of its base. Then move
on to next rectangle.

Is this rectangle within
[A,B]?

Is the difference between areas
of inscribed and circumscribed
rectangles small enough? If
yes, stop computing.

Otherwise, double N, compute
new H and repeat.

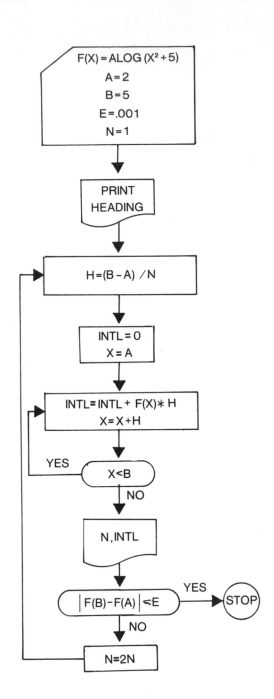

FIGURE 5-5

An integer M is said to be _perfect_ if the sum of all its exact divisors (this includes 1 and M) is 2M. Below we flowchart a search for perfect numbers using this definition. However, we remark that so far as the even perfect numbers are concerned the definition is not the most efficient way to compute them. It has been known[1] for over fifty years that m is an even perfect number if and only if $m = 2^{n-1}(2^n - 1)$ where $2^n - 1$ is a prime. No odd perfect numbers are known. However, it has not yet been proved that there are none.

Let us resist the temptation to start a flowchart until we have analysed the problem a bit. First of all, how will we know if one integer divides another exactly? Recall that in Section 2, when integer arithmetic was discussed, we saw that when an integer M is divided by an integer N, the remainder K is given by K=M-NL, where L is the integer quotient, or, in FORTRAN, K=M-N*(M/N) since M/N is L. Only if K is zero does N divide M exactly. The peculiarities of integer division, therefore, give us an easy way to determine whether or not N divides M.

Next, we ask by what integers M must be divided in order to test it for perfectness? We can rule out testing M itself and require only that the remaining exact divisors have a sum equal to M (rather than twice M). We need not check 1, obviously (though we must remember to add it to the sum of the other divisors). Furthermore, we need not check any integer greater than M/2 (Why not?) Finally, we can rule out any M smaller than six (Why?)[2]

With this preliminary analysis completed we are ready to flow-chart and then program our problem. We denote the integer being checked for perfectness by M and the trial divisor by N. In the following, we use circled numbers to refer to the various elements of our flowchart. The numeral in the floating circle beside each box is the number of that box. The circled numeral at the end of an arrow tells which statement, or group of statements, is to be executed next.

First, we initialize M. Although we know M=6 is perfect, we start with it so that our printout will be complete.

M = 6

①

_____

[1] See, e.g., H.N. Wright, _Theory of Numbers_, John Wiley & Sons, 1939, p. 10.

[2] In the process of assuring ourselves that some perfect numbers exist, we discovered that 6 is the first one.

Initialize N at 2 and ISUM at 1. We put these two operations in a box separate from M=6 so that when we have checked the perfectness of M and move on to M+1, we can reset N to 2 without again using M=6 (Why ISUM rather than SUM?)

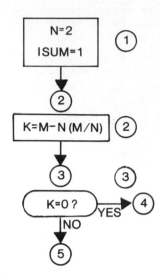

Compute the remainder K, when M is divided by N.

Is the division exact? (In fact, this step and the preceding one can be combined into one interrogation: M−N*(M/N)=0? or M=N*(M/N)?)

If interrogation 3 is answered NO, go directly to box 5 skipping box 4. The next several steps are executed in response to a YES.

If YES, i.e., if N divides M, add N to ISUM and move on to the next trial divisor N+1.

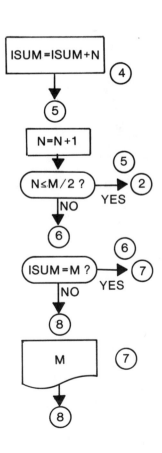

Increment N.
Is the new N less than or equal to M/2? If YES, repeat the operations at and subsequent to box 2.

If NO, we are ready for the crucial question: ISUM=M?

If YES, print M...

...and then increment to the next integer to be tested for perfectness.

...but if NO, increment M without printing it (see box 6).

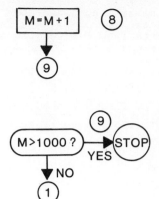

If M is greater than 1,000 we are finished. Otherwise, repeat process.

Putting these all together, we have the flowchart pictured in Figure 5-6. Also in Figure 5-6 is the associated FORTRAN program. Note in particular how the response to interrogation box 3 is handled on the fourth line of the program. Also note the placement of FORMAT. How else might the command to print M have been handled?

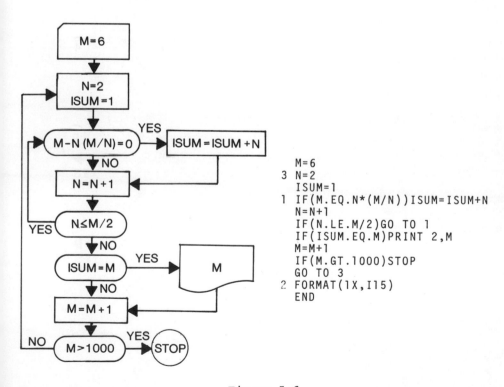

```
  M=6
3 N=2
  ISUM=1
1 IF(M.EQ.N*(M/N))ISUM=ISUM+N
  N=N+1
  IF(N.LE.M/2)GO TO 1
  IF(ISUM.EQ.M)PRINT 2,M
  M=M+1
  IF(M.GT.1000)STOP
  GO TO 3
2 FORMAT(1X,I15)
  END
```

Figure 5-6

No doubt the material which we have just covered is among the most formidable material which the reader has encountered.   The organization of a complicated problem through the use of a flowchart is completely different from earlier "problem solving" techniques. Throughout secondary school mathematics, most "solutions" are the result of applying a "formula" and performing perhaps one or two steps to obtain a result which was always almost visible.   Essentially, no organization was required before starting to compute.

The construction of a flowchart such as in Figure 5-6 is often the result of some experimentation.   Few programmers are so perceptive as to solve (i.e., flowchart) a problem in the most advantageous way on the first attempt.   The final product, if the program is sufficiently important that refinement and documentation is called for, is usually the result of an iteration between the flowchart and the program.   Thus, while the reader is urged to master it, flowcharting is not of such immediate urgency that the one who experiences some difficulty with the EXERCISES at the end of this section need despair.   With continued practice, a measure of skill in flowcharting should come to anyone who is intelligent enough to put on one's hosiery substantially before tying one's shoes.

On the other hand, we do not mean by this that the flowcharting process is of no importance.   Indeed, it is expected that increased insight into the various mathematical processes involved in calculus will be gained through the development and exercise of the processes involved in such "algorithmic" thinking.

A practice which both aids in the mastery of flowcharting and in verifying (up to programming errors) that a flowchart correctly describes the solution to a problem is compute through the flowchart. To do this, set up a table of the names of variables in the various assignment statements in the program and step by step perform the computation required of the computer.   In Figure 5-7   we compute through the flowchart in Figure 5-6.

	M	N	N≤M/2	N divide M?	ISUM	ISUM=M?
Initialize	6	2	–	–	1	–
	6	2	√	√	3	–
	6	3	√	√	6	–
	6	4	NO	–	–	√,PRINT 6
Initialize	7	2	–	–	1	–
	7	2	√	NO	1	–
	7	3	√	NO	1	–
	7	4	NO	–	–	NO

FIGURE 5-7

Another, possibly surprising, feature of the flowcharting of solutions to problems is that more than one solution (i.e., flowchart) is possible. As skill and experience are acquired, the readers flow charts will improve in efficiency and form. In fact, the reader may one day, unbelievably, debate the esthetic virtues of one programming device versus another.

EXERCISES

5-1   Let $F(x) = f(x) \cdot g(x)$ where:

$f(x) = x, \ 0 \le x \le 1$; $g(x) = 8 - x^2, \ 0 \le x \le 2$

$\qquad = 2x - 1, \ 1 < x \le 4$; $= \dfrac{4}{x-1}, \ 2 < x \le 4$.

Write a flowchart to compute and list the values of F from x = 0 to x = 4 at intervals of 0.05.

5-2   Write and run a program based on the flowchart in Exercise 5-1. Hand pick the value of x for which F(x) is largest.

Answer: x = 1.800000E+00, F(1.800000E+00)=1.237600E+01.

5-3   Modify your flowchart in EXERCISE 5-1 to print only the largest value of F and the x which produced it. Run the program.

5-4   Modify the program for Exercise 5-3 to compute the values of

$\dfrac{F(x+h) - F(x)}{h}$ using the value of x determined in Exercise 5-3

and h=±.1,±.01,±.001,±.0001,±.00001,±.000001.

5-5   Consider any integer K. If K is even, divide it by 2 and, if
      the result is 1, stop. If K is odd, multiply it by 3 and add 1.
      The conjecture is that if these alternative steps are repeated
      (iterated) a stop will always be reached after a finite number
      of steps, i.e., the process is conjectured always to reach 1.
      Write a flowchart and program to verify this conjecture for the
      positive integers through 100. For each K(K=1,2,...,100),
      record K and the length of the chain necessary to reach stop.

5-6   Write and run a program to check whether or not an integer p is
      a prime. Run for p = 2n - 1, n = 1,2,3,...,50. Print p when
      it is a prime. When p is not a prime print it and its
      smallest divisor.

5-7   Prime pairs are pairs of primes which differ by 2. Write and
      run a program to print the prime pairs less than 2000.

5-8   A hollow sphere is made of a metal the density of which is
      19.235 lbs/ft³. How much error is made in the weight of a
      sphere whose inside radius is 6 inches if the shell is .018 inch
      thick when it should have been .012 inch thick. Use the
      computer to determine this error (Exercise 2-5) and also
      approximate it using differentials.

5-9   Use the computer to determine the exact value of any quantities
      or errors you found in your calculus text using differentials.

6. Sequences.

The concept of limit, which is fundamental in the study of modern calculus, was developed by Augustin Cauchy during the first quarter of the nineteenth century and helped to put calculus on a rigorous foundation. As great and pervasive as was the work of Newton and Leibnitz, these mathematicians did not possess this important notion. As a result, the validity of their work was questioned for almost two hundred years.

One of the earliest contacts with the notion of limit, for most students, comes in the study of geometric progressions[1] (geometric sequences). There, without knowing that the subject has anything to do with calculus, one is easily persuaded that if the ratio, r, between successive terms, satisfies $|r| < 1$; one can, by taking n large enough, make r^n as near to zero as desired and hence, from the formula $S_n = a(r^n - 1)/(r - 1)$ for the sum of n terms, derive the formula $S = a/(1 - r)$ for the sum of the terms of an infinite geometric progression.

It is not entirely by accident that this kind of limit is one of the first to which the mathematics student is exposed. The geometric progressions provide a class of problems in which sequences of numbers approach a readily computable limit. Furthermore, in these problems, because the limit is known, it is easy to see how well any particular term in the sequence approximates the limit.

The ideas - sequence and limit which we have used above as being intuitively understandable are defined in your calculus text. Except for a few "computer aware" texts of recent genesis, the study of sequences and limits of sequences usually comes relatively late in the typical calculus book. This is not because these topics are difficult or require a knowledge of calculus, but rather because they are directly associated with the study of "infinite series" some of which does require calculus.[2] Divorced from infinite series, sequences

---

[1]A geometric progression in a collection of numbers of the form a, ar, ar^2, ar^3...

[2]Particularly in power series, but also for certain convergence tests in other infinite series.

may be studied at any convenient time. For us that time is now. The
reason is given in the following paragraph.

In many real problems, not ordinarily considered in calculus
courses, it is not possible to write down a solution in any finite
number of steps. Instead, one is forced to consider a sequence of
approximations to a solution. Such a sequence of approximations is
only worthwhile if its quantitative description of the actual solution
improves with each succeeding step. This means that the individual
steps in the sequence of approximations get closer and closer to the
actual solution (and to each other). This leads to the concept of
convergence--that is, the ability to get as close to the actual
solution as we wish, provided we follow the sequence of approximations
far enough.

Much of what we have said above is highly intuitive. To make it
more precise, we now turn to the definitions of sequence and limit
of a sequence and the elementary consequences thereof which are found
in your text.[1] Then, as we would say in FORTRAN:

IF (you are reading this for the <u>second</u> time) skip the next
sentence. After reading about sequences in your text, reread these
intuitive remarks.

In our preliminary study in the calculus text, we have been
mainly concerned with sequences whose terms are given by relatively
simple expressions. In applying these ideas in the study of calculus,
our sequences will occasionally be constructed in somewhat more
complicated ways. Once again Figure 1-5 provides an example. In
that problem we generate for each N (actually only for N = 2,4,8,16,...)
the sum of the areas of a set of inscribed rectangles so that
$\{a_N\}$ = {sum of areas of N rectangles}. Although we never express
this sum in terms of N, the program makes it clear that N uniquely
determines the associated area. Hence, the successive sums are the
terms of a sequence.

Another sequence, a few terms of which we have generated, is seen
in EXERCISE 5-5. Indeed, it is only a conjecture that EXERCISE 5-5
defines a sequence.[2]

---

[1] Some texts, instead of proving theorems on limits of sequences, refer
the reader to proof of theorems about limits of functions. However,
the theorems on limits of sequences can be proved directly from the
definition. Your teacher will indicate the steps.

[2] What if for some K, a 1 is never reached?

Although the concepts of sequence and limit are natural ones, they embody requirements which cannot be met in ordinary computation. The difficulty is that both concepts involve infinite processes. A sequence is an infinite collection of numbers. Clearly, no more than a finite number of them somewhere near the beginning of the sequence can ever be evaluated. To know that L is the limit of a sequence, $\{a_n\}$, requires knowing that $|a_n - L|$ can be made arbitrarily small. Arbitrary smallness cannot be achieved on a computer. Neither can a human achieve arbitrary smallness in computation, but one can conceive of a limiting process and work with this concept in a fruitful way. Indeed, it is a testimonial to the human mind that it is not so limited in the concepts with which it can work.

The smallest numbers which can be represented in a computer are of the order of 10^{-40}. Therefore, the computer cannot distinguish between the two sequences $\{\frac{1}{n} + 10^{-50}\}$ and $\{\frac{1}{n}\}$. While this observation is more theoretical than practical, it is hoped that the student will appreciate the mathematical distinction. In most applications we are content if we can approximate perfection to within some tolerance. If we are only interested in, or only able to distinguish, magnitudes of, say, 10^{-12}, then $\{\frac{1}{n} + 10^{-40}\}$ and $\{\frac{1}{n}\}$ may be thought of as equivalent sequences.

In contrast with actual convergence, we must be content, in computing, with testing whether or not L is approximated by some sequence to within ε for some appropriately small, but not arbitrary, $\varepsilon > 0$. We offer the following definition:

> A sequence $\{a_n\}$ approximates L to within ε if for
> that ε there exists $N(\varepsilon)$ such that $|a_n - L| < \varepsilon$
> when $n > N(\varepsilon)$.

As we have remarked, there is a practical limit to how small ε can be when dealing with a computer.

Much of what we have been discussing is primarily of theoretical interest for one simple reason. All of it assumes that the number L is known. In practical problems, if L is known, the problem is solved. Usually, however, what we want is to find L or some good approximation to it.

In your calculus text are many theorems that assure that sequences formed in various ways do converge. Usually, these theorems are only <u>existence</u> theorems. That is, they tell us that the limit exists but not what the limit is or how to find it. This "theoretical" position is not as useless as it may appear at first glance because the <u>knowledge that the limit does exist gives us a good reason to try to approximate it</u>.

We state here three such theorems which will be of considerable use to us.

<u>Theorem A</u>: A monotonic[1] sequence is convergent if and only if it is bounded.[2]

<u>Theorem B</u>: Let $\{a_n\}$ and $\{c_n\}$ be respectively monotone increasing and monotone decreasing sequences. For each k, let $c_k > a_n$ and $c_n > a_k$ for every n > 0. Then $\{a_n\}$ and $\{c_n\}$ both converge.

<u>Theorem C</u>: (The squeeze theorem)

Suppose $\{a_n\}$, $\{b_n\}$, $\{c_n\}$ are such that:

1) For each k, $c_k > a_n$ and $c_n > a_k$ for all n,

2) $\{a_n\}$ and $\{c_n\}$ are monotone increasing and decreasing, respectively, to the common limit L,

3) $a_n < b_n < c_n$ for all n, then, $\{b_n\}$ also converges to L.

It is obvious that this theorem can be generalized by omitting the requirement of monotonicity on $\{a_n\}$ and $\{c_n\}$.

Figure 1-5 gives an example of the use of the squeeze theorem. In that problem we wished to find the "area"[3] bounded by the graphs of y = 0, y = $\log(x^2 + 5)$, x = 2 and x = 5. To find this area we generated sequences which were sums of areas of rectangles each with base of length 3/N. Figure 6-1 shows a typical rectangle. In it we seek the area of the region ABFC. The rectangle ABDC is entirely contained in the region whose area we seek; ABEF entirely contains this region. If we sum the areas of all such rectangles (See Figures 5-1 and 5-2) and denote the sum of the areas of the rectangles

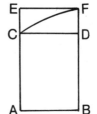

[1]A sequence is <u>monotone increasing</u> if $a_{n+1} > a_n$ and is <u>monotone decreasing</u> if $a_{n+1} < a_n$ for all n. A sequence which is either monotone increasing or montone decreasing is said to be <u>monotonic</u>.

[2]A sequence is said to be bounded if there is an M such that $|a_n| < M$ for all n.

[3]The notion of area for figures other than those used in geometry, e.g., rectangles and triangles, is made precise by the theory of the definite integral.

in Figure 5-1. by C_N and those in Figure 5-2 by A_N, then we not only have $A_N \leq C_N$ but, if we denote the actual area described above by B_N (B_N is a constant), we also have $A_N \leq B_N \leq C_N$.

What is also apparent, although we shall not prove it at this time, is that with increasing N, A_N increases and C_N decreases monotonically. We must also defer a discussion of actual convergence of these sequences. Their convergence will be proved in the detailed study of the definite integral in your text. However, running the program in Figure 1-5 reveals that $|A_N - C_N| < .001$ for $N > 4096$. Assuming that monotonicity and convergence to, say, L can be proved, this result shows that both the sequence $\{A_N\}$ and the sequence $\{C_N\}$ approximate L to within .001. L is, of course, B_N. In Figure 1-5 we chose to print only the elements of A_N.

A geometric interpretation of EXERCISE 5-4 involving the "squeeze theorem" may also be given but this is left as an exercise for the reader.

Occasionally, one encounters situations in which no bound is known for a monotone increasing sequence. When, in such situations, the differences between successive terms can be made arbitrarily small one may be tempted to infer convergence. Such inference is filled with peril as the following example shows.

Consider the sequence:

$h_1 = 1$

$h_2 = 1 + 1/2$

$h_3 = 1 + 1/2 + 1/3$

$h_4 = 1 + 1/2 + 1/3 + 1/4$

$\vdots$

$h_n = 1 + 1/2 + 1/3 + 1/4 + ... + 1/n$.

Since the difference between h_{n+1} and h_n is $\frac{1}{n+1}$, it is clear that the difference between successive terms can be made arbitrarily small. However, $\{h_n\}$ diverges! Its terms eventually become larger than any preassigned number although their growth is deceptively slow.

It can be shown that $h_n \doteq \ln n$ for large n.[1] Therefore, for $h_n \geq 15$, say, n must be at least 20^5. Some idea of the rate of this

_____

[1]The difference $h_n - \ln n$ approaches .5772... . This is called Euler's number.

divergence is seen by visualizing an individual who computes one new term of $\{h_n\}$ in every minute of an eight-hour working day. In order for our diligent computer to reach $h_n = 15$, over 25 working years would be required. This example shows something of the practical importance of the squeeze theorem. Unfortunately, we must sometimes attempt to approximate limits which we do not know to exist. Some current scholars in numerical analysis are researching demonstrations, which while falling short of traditional mathematical proofs, will "convince reasonable men of the correctness of ones results" (J. R. Rice quoted from ONR Pasadena Monthly Activity Report, January 1971).

We do not wish to imply that when we cannot actually find the limit, L, of a sequence nor apply the squeeze theorem nothing can be said about convergence. Although it is not of utility in computing, there is a convergence criterion which can be applied, at least theoretically. This is due to Cauchy and states:

A sequence $\{a_n\}$ converges if and only if given any $\varepsilon > 0$ there is an N such that if $n > N$ then $|a_{n+m} - a_n| < \varepsilon$ for all positive integers m.

In both Figure 1-5 and EXERCISE 5-4 the terms of $\{a_n\}$ and $\{c_n\}$ are generated independently of each other. In applying computer generated sequences and the squeeze theorem to the solution of problems, this is not always the case. An example is afforded by a technique for finding a unique root, r, of $f(x) = 0$ between a and b when we know that $f(a) \cdot f(b) < 0$.[1] Our technique is to find the midpoint, c, of (a,b) and ask which of $f(a) \cdot f(c)$, $f(c) \cdot f(b)$ is negative. This gives us a new interval containing the root, r, and we repeat these operations until r is known to be in an interval of suitable length. The succeeding left and right hand end points of intervals containing r form the monotone increasing and decreasing sequences (unless we should experience the serendipity of actually finding a root as the midpoint of some interval). Clearly the terms of these two sequences need not be determined by any alternating manner (see Figure 6-2).

The planning necessary to write a program such as that in Figure 1-5, or to write a program to find a root of $f(x) = 0$ introduces a kind of algorithm quite different from those necessary to do the

---

[1] We assume that f takes on every value between $f(a)$ and $f(b)$. That is, there must then be an $r \in (a,b)$ such that $f(r) = 0$. This is a consequence of continuity.

$\{a_n\}$	L	R	$\{c_n\}$
a_1	2	3	c_1
a_2	2.5	3	
a_3	2.75	3	
a_4	2.875	3	
	2.875	2.9375	c_2
a_5	2.90625	2.9375	
a_6	2.921875	2.9375	
	2.921875	2.9291875	c_3
$\vdots$	$\vdots$	$\vdots$	$\vdots$

Figure 6-2

problems in Section 5. All of the algorithms in that section might be called finite algorithms while those of the present section would more properly be called infinite algorithms.[1] In each case we have truncated the algorithm by requiring only approximation to within ε. This truncation is necessary for computing. The algorithms themselves, freed of this practical necessity, describe sequences which converge to the numbers the computer approximates.

We now turn to some questions of the mechanics of computing with sequences.

Because a sequence has an infinite set of what may be distinct values, it may appear, initially, that the programmer and the compiler must solve the formidable problem of providing storage space for these values and providing a way to identify the associated integer from the domain of the sequence. This is usually not the case. In the first place, most applications only require computing a few terms near the beginning of the sequence. Then, second, once we have obtained a new element of a sequence, improving our knowledge of the limit, we are usually free to discard previous terms. Of course, if we wish to have these elements for reference, we can cause them to be printed as generated but need not store them in the computer's memory. However, in Section 9 (Subscripts) we discuss how a finite number of them may be stored if that is desired.

---

[1]Again see Rice and Rice.

Those cases in which we must retain some elements of a sequence in the computer's memory usually involve sequences which are defined recursively. That is, sequences in which each element is expressed in terms of some finite set of preceding elements.

To illustrate, we discuss a sequence which the reader may find interesting. It is, incidentally, a sequence which does not converge. The sequence is called Fibonacci's sequence after a 12th century mathematician who worked with it, although it is probably of earlier origin. This sequence is often said to have resulted from the following problem:[1]

> Suppose that a pair of rabbits is productive from
> the second month on, that each productive pair
> produces a pair of rabbits (one each male and
> female) every month, that deaths do not occur
> (this is no more unlikely than the rest of it).
> How many pairs of rabbits exist after n months?

It is easy to see that the first few terms are: $1,1,2,3,5,8,13\cdots$ Furthermore, it is not difficult to verify that the successive elements of the sequence are defined by the recurrence relation:

$$a_n = a_{n-1} + a_{n-2}; \quad a_1 = 1, \quad a_2 = 1 .$$

Our interest here is in writing a flowchart from which a program can be written to compute these successive elements without storing any of them longer than necessary. In this program we use the names AN, ANMIN1 and ANMIN2 for a_n, a_{n-1} and a_{n-2}, respectively. In the flowchart we have provided for stopping after N achieves some value K. This is required to prevent exceeding the maximum allowable size of numbers.

The device of using a stored value and then replacing it with a more recently determined element as we have in the last two computing boxes in Figure 6-3 is frequently useful in computations involving sequences.

---

[1] See also Volume 1 of The World of Mathematics by James R. Newman, Simon and Schuster, 1956. In this reference other sources of the sequence and instances of its occurrence in nature are given.

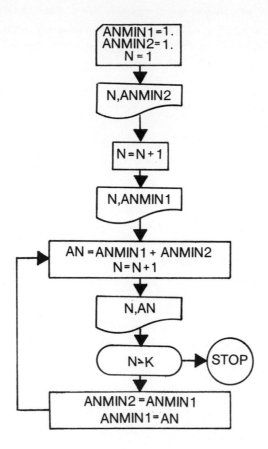

Figure 6-3

With this final caution concerning computing we leave this
section. Such repetitive computations as we have described above are
called loops (because of the appearance of their flowcharts). When
operating a computer, we always want these loops to be traversed only
a finite number of times. In order to avoid the possibility that,
because of extremely slow convergence or an error, our program might
run beyond all reasonable time limits, the reader is reminded (See
e.g. EXERCISE 3-3(b)) that it is usually a good idea to insert a
computation which counts the number of times the loop has been
traversed and terminates computation after some reasonable number of
times. There are other reasons for terminating a program on the basis
of the number of times a loop is traversed which we will discuss
further when we consider roundoff error.

EXERCISES

6-1   Flowchart the process described for finding a root, r, of
      $f(x) = 0$.   Provide for stopping if an actual root is discovered.
      Provide for stopping if the loop has been traversed more than
      16 times.   Provide for printing r.   Run your program for
      $f(x) = \sin x + 3 \cos x$, $a = \pi/2$, $b = \pi$.

6-2   Methods of approximation in which one guesses a solution and
      uses a formula to produce a better guess, etc., are called
      recursive methods.   One such is a standard method of finding
      square roots.   To find $\sqrt{a}$, make a guess x_0.   If $x_0 < \sqrt{a}$,
      $(a/x_0) > \sqrt{a}$, and conversely.   In either case, average x_0 and
      a/x_0.   Call this x_1. x_1 is greater than x_0 and smaller than
      $\sqrt{a}/x_0$ or vice versa.   Continuing, we develop the algorithm
      (See also Exercise 3-2(i)):

$$x_{n+1} = (x_n + a/x_n)/2.$$

      Write a flowchart to use the algorithm to find $\sqrt{a}$.   Stop when
      $|x_n - \frac{a}{x_n}| < \varepsilon$ or $n > 20$.   Output x_n if the first criterion is
      met, a if the second is met.   Does the flowchart describe your
      program for Exercise 3-3(a)?

6-3   Based on your flowchart in EXERCISE 6-2, write a program to
      approximate the square roots of .5, 2, 75 and 500 to within
      10^{-4}.   Because of the speed of the computer, it is not
      important to make a good first guess.   One can always start
      with 1 or with a, itself.   For each a, print the number of
      approximations required and the final x_n.   Also, print $\sqrt{a}$
      as given by the FORTRAN function SQRT.

6-4   Sequences which do not converge can also be of interest.   Write
      a program to generate the two sequences:

$$(X_0, X_1, \cdots, X_n, \cdots) \quad \text{and} \quad (Y_0, Y_1, \cdots, Y_n, \cdots)$$

      where

$$X_0 = Y_0 = 68.7$$
$$X_{n+1} = 2X_n \text{EXP}(-.01Y_n)$$
$$Y_{n+1} = 2X_n - X_{n+1}$$

Compute the first 50 terms and observe fluctuations in the values of X_n. Repeat the computation with:

$$X_0 = Y_0 = 100 \ \text{ALOG}(2)$$

(This is a model for host (X) and parasite (Y) population densities in the nth generation. It is based on a problem in the book by J. Maynard Smith, <u>Mathematical Ideas in Biology</u>, Cambridge University Press, Cambridge, 1968.)

6-5   Although a computer cannot be used to evaluate limits, its careful use sometimes provides experimental evidence of the value of a limit. By use of a computer, or other means, evaluate the following for $x \in \{10^{-n}\}$, $n = 1, 2, \ldots, 20$.

    (a) $\lim_{x \to 0} (1 + x)^{1/x}$;

    (b) $\lim_{x \to +\infty} (1 + \frac{1}{x})^x$;

    (c) $\lim_{x \to 0} \frac{\sin x}{x}$;

    (d) $\lim_{x \to 0} x^{x^2}$.

6-6   Use Newton's method to find where, between $x = \frac{\pi}{2}$ and $x = \pi$, $7e^{-x}\sin x = .7853982$.

6-7   Approximately what is the relative maximum value of $e^{-1/x}\log x$ between $x = .1/2$ and $x = 1$? Use a numerical method to solve $f'(x) = 0$.

6-8   Repeat EXERCISE 6-5 for
    (a) $\lim_{x \to 0} \sin(1/x)$
    (b) $\lim_{x \to 0} x^2\sin(1/x)$

6-9   What values do you think the functions in EXERCISE 6-5 (a), (c) and (d) and EXERCISE 6-8 should have at $x = 0$ to be continuous there?

7. Output Formatting.

Thus far we have been content with the simplified, but rigid, output statement described in Section 2. However, FORTRAN provides much more versatile and useful output capabilities. Using these, the programmer may specify precisely which and how many printing spaces are to be occupied by his output[1]. Within the limitations of the character set[2] available on the printer, the programmer may also cause the computer to write appropriate words, sentences and other symbols. Thus, FORTRAN provides the capability of arranging the output of a program in tabular form, such as Figure 7-3, page 7-72, complete with titles.

Depending upon the compiler, several FORTRAN statements may be available to cause the computer to print the results of computation. The American Standards Institute specifies that a statement of the form WRITE (n,k), perhaps followed by a list of variables, be available. n refers to the output unit to be used. Its value is determined by the Computer Center. Usually, the line printer is known as unit 6. In this case we would have WRITE (6,k). (The card punch is usually unit 5. We will not require punched card output in this course.) As in Section 2, k links WRITE with its associated FORMAT statement. An alternate output statement, available on some compilers, is the statement used in Section 2, PRINT k, followed by a list of variables. Less frequently available are the unformatted[3] output statements WRITE(n) and PRINT. These do not utilize the specifications of a FORMAT statement, the compiler being designed to output data according

[1]Such specifications must be compatible with the size of the numbers represented and the maximum number of digits allowed by the computer. On the IBM 7094 the maximum number of digits allowed for a real constant is 9 including the decimal point and for an integer constant the maximum number of digits allowed is 11. On the CDC 6500 these numbers are 15 and 18 respectively.

[2]The symbols specified by US Standard FORTRAN are: A,B,C,D,E,F,G,H,I, J,K,L,M,N,O,P,Q,R,S,T,U,V,W,X,Y,Z,0,1,2,3,4,5,6,7,8,9,~(blank),=,+,-, *,/,(,),.,$, and comma. Some others may be available locally.

[3]Computer scientists use "unformatted" in two ways. (a) Not requiring a FORMAT statement, (b) Not converted from the internal (binary) code of the computer. The former is intended here.

to type and size. The unformatted PRINT will not be of further
interest in this section since the exploitation of FORMAT is our
primary interest. In what follows we use PRINT k to elicit output.

Before embarking upon this study, we remark that the practice of
placing the FORMAT statement immediately after the associated PRINT
statement is not required. All FORMAT statements may be placed
together just before the END card if desired. This has the advantage
of not cluttering the program with FORMATs which merely tells the
computer how to respond to PRINTs. FORMATs may even precede their
associated PRINT statements but all FORMAT statements must be preceded
by some executable statement.

Our experience with the output instructions given in Section 2
tells us that outputting an integer is signalled by the symbol I and
a real is signalled by the symbol E. The numerals following these
sysmbols established 15 printing spaces for each type of number with
all the digits appearing in the right-most spaces. The numerals output are said to be right justified with respect to these printing
spaces. I15 and E15.n are called field descriptors. 15 is called the
field width. As we observe, the field width can be greater than the
number of digits output. Clearly, it cannot be smaller. In general,
the numeral 15, used in Section 2, may be replaced with any convenient
numeral and n is not restricted to values of 6 or less. The general
form of these field descriptors then becomes Ip and Em.n. In the
former, if p is smaller than the number of digits in the output integer
only the right most digits are output. Many compilers signal this
deficiency by an initial *. In the latter, m must provide for n
decimal places, an initial zero, a decimal point, a sign, the symbol E
and three spaces for the signed exponent. Thus, $m \geq n + 7$ is required.
The choice of m and p is often made to achieve a desirable spacing in
output.

It should not be supposed that the field width provision of
FORTRAN output has anything to do with the size of numbers or the
number of digits which can be output. These matters are determined by
the combination of the hardware/software package provided by the Center.
For example, on the IBM 7094 and CDC 6500 we must have $n \leq 9$ and $n \leq 15$
respectively. We have previously remarked that an integer can have
no more than 11 and 18 digits, respectively, on these machines.

As will have been suspected from the FORMAT statements in
Figure 1-5, other capabilities exist. Line 32 suggests that other
field descriptors exist and lines 16 and 17 suggest that appropriately

spaced table heading can be produced by the program itself.

We next introduce the field descriptor Fm.n used in Figure 1-5. Fm.n specifies real number output in standard (i.e. not exponential) notation.   As in the E descriptor, m specifies the total number of printing spaces to be used and n specifies the number of decimal places.   In this notation m must exceed n by 3, the spaces required for a sign, at least one digit to the left of the decimal point and the decimal point.   However, determining m in an F descriptor is a little more complicated than in the case of E because it must also account for the size of the real being output.   As in the case of the I descriptor, if m - (n+3) places are too few to accomodate the integer part of the real number, it will be truncated of its left most, i.e. most significant part, in printing.   Again, some compilers signal this truncation with an asterisk before the left-most digit. Obviously, the F field descriptor is not appropriate for outputting very large or very small numbers.

Another field descriptor of considerable utility is the skip descriptor pX.   Its effect is to skip p columns in the printed output. It is used to space out printed material so as to create an aesthetically pleasing printed page.   On line 16 of Figure 1-5, 6X provides six blank spaces between WHEN THE NUMBER OF RECTANGLES IS and THE APPROXIMATION TO THE AREA IS.   The 1X on the same line avoids printing in the first column.   Further on we discuss the effect of the first column on the output.   On line 32 of Figure 1-5, the specifications are 14X,I6,30X,F7.3.   In order, these cause the printer to skip over 14 columns, print the digits of an integer variable (N) in the right-most of the next six columns, skip over the next 30 columns and finally print a real variable (INTL) with three decimal places in the next seven columns.   The choices of p and m were based on the programmers estimate of the magnitudes of the numbers to be output.   The choice of n was dictated by the accuracy which the program was asked to achieve.   The field descriptors in a list must be separated from each other by commas.

The spacing prescribed by the FORMAT statement on line 32 of Figure 1-5 could be achieved in other ways.   One would be to replace line 32 by

    3 FORMAT(I20,F37.3)

which combines the 14X,I6 descriptors, still printing the integer N in the right most of these 20 spaces and which combines the descriptors 30X, F7.3, similarly.   There is no particular reason to prefer one of these sets of field descriptors over another except for keypunch (typing) considerations.

It is not necessary for every PRINT statement to have its own FORMAT statement. If two or more PRINT statements have lists of the same length with variables of the same type arranged in the same order, the same FORMAT statement may be used for all. For example, a program might contain the following:

```
        .
        .
        .
    PRINT 101,X,ITEM,Y
        .
        .
        .
    PRINT 101,SUM,JIG,REM
        .
        .
        .
    PRINT 101,VAT,ICOUNT,DIFF
        .
        .
        .
101 FORMAT(1X,F10.3,I6,F15.6)
    END
```

If a PRINT list contains q consecutive variables with identical field descriptors, say F10.7 in the case of q reals, the notation qF10.7 assigns the same specifications to each and obviates the need to write F10.7 q times. The I and E specifications are handled in the same way. If a block of descriptors repeats r times the block may be enclosed in parentheses preceded by r. For example, 3(I3,F7.3) is the same as I3,F7.3,I3,F7.3,I3,F7.3. This is different, of course, from 3I3,3F7.3 which is I3,I3,I3,F7.3,F7.3,F7.3.

As we have suggested and, as in exemplified by the program in Figure 1-5, the labels for the output of a program may be included in the program as they are on lines 15, 16 and 17 of that figure. We first discuss a procedure which is widely available. However, because it exceeds the specifications of the American Standards Institute, it may not exist in every installation. Therefore, at the conclusion of this part of the Section, we describe a modified procedure which is specified by the Standard.

To write[1] any collection of words or symbols (in the available character set), other than the values of variables stored in the computer, the statements:

---

[1]Not available in SBF.

```
      PRINT k
    k FORMAT('...words and symbols...')
```

are used. Here k serves the same purpose as before and needs no
further discussion. The quote signs within the parentheses delineate
the beginning and ending of the words and symbols to be printed,
together with their desired spacing. The output produced by these
statements will be: ...words and symbols... As remarked above, an
example is found on lines 15, 16 and 17 of Figure 1-5.

It occasionally happens that the programmer wishes to print only
a few widely spaced words. For example, column headings such as IN,
OUT and TIME centered above six-digit columns, the first indented 1
space and the succeeding ones separated by 10 spaces could be called
for by the statements:

```
      PRINT 100
  100 FORMAT('~~~IN~~~~~~~~~~~~~~OUT~~~~~~~~~~~~TIME')
```

where ~ indicates a blank. In this application, blank is a valid
FORTRAN symbol.

An alternative to this notation uses the skipping symbol pX
between words. Using this, the above statements would become:

```
      PRINT 100
  100 FORMAT(3X,'IN',14X,'OUT',12X,'TIME')
```

In either case, the output would have the form

```
   IN                OUT              TIME
```

The second form as the advantage of simplicity and avoids the
possibility of an inadvertent misspacing and a resultant misalignment
of column headings due to an inaccurate count of the blanks. Note
the use of commas. They separate the skipping specifications from
the symbol specifications.

The versatility of the FORTRAN output capabilities is shown by
combining the above output techniques. If in Figure 1-5 it had been
desired to write repeated lines of the form:

```
WHEN THE NUMBER OF RECTANGLES IS    1, THE APPROXIMATION TO THE AREA IS  6.592
```

for the successive values of N and INTL rather than using the columnar
format, the programmer could have eliminated lines 15, 16 and 17 of
Figure 1-5 and in place of lines 31 and 32 written:

```
      PRINT 3,N,INTL
    3 FORMAT(1X,'WHEN THE NUMBER OF RECTANGLES IS',I6,',','THE APPROXIM
     1ATION TO THE AREA IS',F7.3)
```

As before, the specifications of printing spaces for numeric portion of output must be in the same order as in the PRINT list. Also, note that the numeric specifications must be separated from the '...words and symbols...' by commas. The skip symbol pX may also be incorporated in such a FORMAT specification when desired.

A remark is now in order concerning the location in the program of the various PRINT and FORMAT statements. A little reflection will reveal why the two PRINT, FORMAT statements are located as they are in Figure 1-5. The first, on lines 15, 16 and 17, is to be executed but once and, hence, must not be part of any loop and must precede the second. It could, therefore, be anywhere before the statement numbered 4 (line 20) and after the definition of F(X) (since PRINT is executable). On the other hand, the second PRINT, FORMAT pair is to be executed each time new values of both N and INTL are computed. It must, then, be part of the loop where they are computed and subsequent to the statements which assign them their values.

As we remarked earlier, the technique which we have just described for printing table headings, etc. is not part of the American Standards Institute FORTRAN. However, a reasonable alternative is provided[1]. The Standard provides for the H (Hollerith) field descriptor. The descriptor pH, where p is an integer, calls for verbatim printing of the p characters, including blanks, which follow the H. In this notation our first example becomes

```
      PRINT 100
  100 FORMAT(38H~~~IN~~~~~~~~~~~~~OUT~~~~~~~~~~~~TIME)
```

The count of total spaces required must be accurate. For example, 37H rather than 38H would result in TIME being printed as TIM. The alternate form becomes

```
      PRINT 100
  100 FORMAT(3X,2HIN,14X,3HOUT,12X,4HTIME)
```

Lines 15 and 16 of Figure 1-5 would become

```
    1 FORMAT(1X,32HWHEN THE NUMBER OF RECTANGLES IS,6X,32HTHE APPROXIMAT
    1ION TO THE AREA IS,//)
```

We now turn to a discussion of vertical control.

Ordinarily, when a PRINT statement is encountered, the paper automatically rolls up one line and prints the specified output. This action is provided for by the compiler. Other vertical carriage control codes allow the programmer to move the paper up other

_____
[1]Neither is available in SBF.

specified numbers of lines. These controls utilize the first printing column which so far we have scrupulously avoided through the use of the skip descriptor 1X.

To activate these controls, the programmer utilizes the first position in the line to "write" the control character. This character is not printed. It is used only for control. The control characters are given in Table 7-1.

TABLE 7-1

Control Character[1]		Response
'~' or 1H~ (i.e., blank)		Space up one line[2].
'0'	1H0	Space up an additional line, i.e., double space.
'1'	1H1	Space to the top of the next page.
'+'	1H+	Suppress spacing.

An additional and very useful code for advancing paper is / (slant). Within[3] a FORMAT specification, its use signals the end of a printed line (end of record). Such use causes the remainder of the output specified to be printed on the next (or succeeding) line. // (double slant) calls for a line to be skipped before continuing with the output specified. /// skips two lines, etc. It is not necessary to separate / from other field descriptors by commas.

The combination of / at the end of a FORMAT specification and a succeeding PRINT statement gives a slightly different output. The / causes the paper to advance. PRINT also causes the paper to advance. The combination, therefore, leads to double spacing. An example of the use of slant is found on line 17 of Figure 1-5 where // followed by PRINT (line 31) leaves two blank lines between the heading and the numerical output. Other examples follow.

Task:

Suppose that we have computed the daily average values of the quantities POL, HUM, VIS, CLD, PRECP and the values are respectively 37 gr., 85%, 12 miles, 26%, .05 inches for the 212th day of the year. Using a single FORMAT statement, output these so as to produce the table.

---

[1]Not available in SBF.

[2]' ' has the same effect as PRINT alone. Its main purpose is to avoid an inadvertent carriage advance when writing words and symbols. Using 1X as the first symbol in the FORMAT specification will also avoid this problem.

[3]Naturally, a / between quote marks will simply be printed. It has no spacing effect in this case.

```
LIFE VALUES ON THE 212TH DAY OF 1977
        POL   = 37 GR.
        HUM   = 85. PERCENT
        VIS   = 12. MILES
        CLD   = 26. PERCENT
        PRECP = .05 INCHES
```

Program: (Segment)

```
    PRINT 1,DAY IPOL,HUM,VIS,CLD,PRECP
  1 FORMAT(1X,'LIFE VALUES ON THE ',I3,'TH DAY OF 1977.'/6X,'POL   = '
  1,I2,' GR.'/'HUM   = ',F3.0/'VIS   = ',F3.0/'CLD   = ',F3.0,'PRECP
  2= ',F3.2)
```

Another output capability is sometimes useful. It is the
capability of the printer to output lines of up to 132 characters[1].
Hence, output FORMAT's may call for the printing of 132 spaces and
characters. Using this capability often requires that FORMAT statements be continued over several cards. For example, the output of
an accounting system setting charges for equipment usage could include
the following statements:

```
    PRINT 100
100 FORMAT(IX,'MEMBER CODE',5X,'TIME OUT',5X,'TIME IN',5X,'TOTAL TIME'
  1,5X,'COST PER HOUR',5X,'TIME SINCE LAST USE',5X,'PENALTY PER HOUR'
  2,5X,'CHARGE'//)
    PRINT 101,ITEM,TO,TI,TT,CPH,TLU,PEN,CHARGE
101 FORMAT(I8,F14.2,F13.2,F14.2,F16.2,F23.2,F21.2,F16.2/)
```

Studying examples of programs is a way to become familiar with
the uses of the various techniques which we have been discussing.
The reader may wish to refer back to some of the foregoing examples
while preparing new programs.   In addition, we give several
additional examples to conclude this section. One of these, a table
of compound interest, is discussed further in the EXERCISES at the
end of this section.

Figure 7-1 lists a program embodying many of the carriage control
codes discussed in this section. A little ingenuity should enable
the programmer to use these codes to meet most of his output needs.
In studying it, comparison with Figure 7-2 is suggested.

1) Lines 1, 2 and 3 print the heading. Note the two ways / is
    utilized.

2) On line 2 the '1' starts the printout at the top of a page.

---

[1]This figure varies with the printer. The one given is for the
IBM 1401.

3) Note how the lines following the first comment allow for outputting the two forms 8/9 and 1/10.

4) Note, in the sixth comment (eighth and ninth comment cards) how printing 2/4, for example, is avoided.

```
      PRINT 10
   10 FORMAT('1','SEVEN PLACE DECIMAL EQUIVALENTS OF FRACTIONS'
     1/15X,'(1/2 TO 11/12)'//)
      N=1
      M=2
    2 DEC=FLOAT(N)/FLOAT(M)
C  NEXT FOUR CARDS ALLOW EITHER ONE OR TWO PRINTING SPACES FOR
C  M AS APPROPRIATE
      IF(M.GT.9)GO TO 12
      PRINT 11,N,M,DEC
   11 FORMAT(13X,I2,'/',I1,F14.7)
      GO TO 17
   12 PRINT 13,N,M,DEC
   13 FORMAT(13X,I2,'/',I2,F13.7)
C  INCREASE NUMERATOR BY ONE UNLESS THIS CAUSES IT TO EXCEED
C  THE DENOMINATOR
   17 N=N+1
      IF(N.GT.M-1)GO TO 14
      GO TO 1
C  NOW INCREMENT M AND START OVER
   14 M=M+1
      N=1
C  WHEN M EXCEEDS 12 STOP
      IF(M.GT.12)GO TO 16
C  OTHERWISE SPACE UP ONE SPACE FOR NEXT DENOMINATOR SET
      PRINT 15
   15 FORMAT(' ')
C  THE NEXT TEN CARDS CHECK WHETHER THE NEW N/M HAS BEEN
C  PREVIOUSLY COMPUTED
    1 K=1
      L=2
   19 IF(N*L.EQ.K*M)GO TO 17
      K=K+1
      IF(K.EQ.L)GO TO 18
      GO TO 19
   18 L=L+1
      K=1
      IF(L.GE.M)GO TO 2
      GO TO 19
C  THIS PUTS COMPUTING CENTER NOTES ON A SEPARATE SHEET
   16 PRINT 20
   20 FORMAT('1')
      STOP
      END
```

Figure 7-1

SEVEN PLACE DECIMAL EQUIVALENTS OF FRACTIONS
(1/2 TO 11/12)

1/2	0.5000000
1/3	0.3333333
2/3	0.6666667
1/4	0.2500000
3/4	0.7500000
1/5	0.2000000
2/5	0.4000000
3/5	0.6000000
4/5	0.8000000
1/6	0.1666667
5/6	0.8333333
1/7	0.1428571
2/7	0.2857143
3/7	0.4285714
4/7	0.5714286
5/7	0.7142857
6/7	0.8571429
1/8	0.1250000
3/8	0.3750000
5/8	0.6250000
7/8	0.8750000
1/9	0.1111111
2/9	0.2222222
4/9	0.4444444
5/9	0.5555556
7/9	0.7777778
8/9	0.8888889
1/10	0.1000000
3/10	0.3000000
7/10	0.7000000
9/10	0.9000000
1/11	0.0909091
2/11	0.1818182
3/11	0.2727273
4/11	0.3636364
5/11	0.4545455
6/11	0.5454545
7/11	0.6363636
8/11	0.7272727
9/11	0.8181818
10/11	0.9090909
1/12	0.0833333
5/12	0.4166667
7/12	0.5833333
11/12	0.9166667

Output of program in Figure 7-1

Figure 7-2

The following Table, Figure 7-3, is the result of a single computer program. See EXERCISE 7-1.

THE FUTURE AMOUNT OF $1.00

INTEREST AT 6. PERCENT COMPOUNDED

YEAR	SEMIANNUALLY	QUARTERLY	MONTHLY
1	1.060900	1.061363	1.061678
2	1.125509	1.126492	1.127160
3	1.194052	1.195618	1.196680
4	1.266770	1.268985	1.270489
5	1.343916	1.346855	1.348850
6	1.425761	1.429502	1.432044
7	1.512589	1.517221	1.520369
8	1.604706	1.610323	1.614142
9	1.702433	1.709138	1.713699
10	1.806111	1.814017	1.819396

INTEREST AT 7. PERCENT COMPOUNDED

YEAR	SEMIANNUALLY	QUARTERLY	MONTHLY
1	1.071225	1.071859	1.072290
2	1.147523	1.148882	1.149806
3	1.229255	1.231439	1.232926
4	1.316809	1.319929	1.322054
5	1.410599	1.414778	1.417625
6	1.511069	1.516443	1.520105
7	1.618694	1.625413	1.629994
8	1.733986	1.742213	1.747826
9	1.857489	1.867407	1.874177
10	1.989789	2.001597	2.009661

INTEREST AT 8. PERCENT COMPOUNDED

YEAR	SEMIANNUALLY	QUARTERLY	MONTHLY
1	1.081600	1.082432	1.082999
2	1.169859	1.171659	1.172888
3	1.265319	1.268242	1.270237
4	1.368569	1.372786	1.375666
5	1.480244	1.485947	1.489845
6	1.601032	1.608437	1.613502
7	1.731676	1.741024	1.747422
8	1.872981	1.884540	1.892457
9	2.025816	2.039887	2.049529
10	2.191123	2.208039	2.219639

Figure 7-3

The LISTING and OUTPUT below gives a further example of a table heading created by a FORMAT statement.

LISTING:

```
    PRINT 3
  3 FORMAT('1','VOLUME OF THE PURDUE WATER TANK BY FOOT FROM THE LOW W
   1ATER LINE'//4X,'(BASED ON THE ASSUMPTION THAT THE BOUNDARY, IN ELE
   2VATION,'/17X,'IS A CIRCLE OF RADIUS 21.158 FT '/4X,'WITH CENTER ON
   3 THE EQUATOR 25.998 FT FROM THE CENTER LINE'/5X,'AND SCALED TO 1,5
   400,000 GALLONS AT A DEPTH OF 35 FEET)'///10X,'WATER DEPTH',27X,'VO
   5LUME'/1X,'(IN FEET ABOVE THE LOW WATER LINE)', 4X,'(IN THOUSANDS O
   6F GALLONS)'//)
```

OUTPUT

VOLUME OF THE PURDUE WATER TANK BY FOOT FROM THE LOW WATER LINE

(BASED ON THE ASSUMPTION THAT THE BOUNDARY, IN ELEVATION,
IS A CIRCLE OF RADIUS 21.158 FT
WITH CENTER ON THE EQUATOR 25.998 FT FROM THE CENTER LINE
AND SCALED TO 1,500,000 GALLONS AT A DEPTH OF 35 FEET)

WATER DEPTH (IN FEET ABOVE THE LOW WATER LINE)	VOLUME (IN THOUSANDS OF GALLONS)

EXERCISES

7-1   Write a program to produce the output listed in Figure 7-3. The formula for computing compound interest is:

$$A = P(1 + r/n)^{nk}$$

where P is the number of dollars invested

         r is the annual interest rate

         n is the number of times per year interest is computed

         k is the number of years interest is accumulated on P (no interest is withdrawn)

         A is number of dollars P grows to under the conditions described by r, n, k

7-2   Investigate effect of more frequent compounding of interest by extending Figure 7-3 to include WEEKLY, DAILY, HOURLY and MINUTELY compounding intervals. For the purposes of this problem, change the interest rates to 4%, 6%, 8% and 10%.

7-3   What formula gives the result of compounding interest continuously?

7-4   Rewrite EXERCISE 4-2 so that the output has the heading
       "A=ANGLE 1, B=ANGLE 2, C=ANGLE 3". Then output the computed
       values of the angles in the form:

           ANGLE 1 =
           ANGLE 2 =
           ANGLE 3 =

7-5   Consider the region R: 0 ≤ x ≤ 2
       0 ≤ y ≤ 3 subdivided into 60
       triangles as in the sketch.
       Write and run a program to
       compute and print the coordinates
       of the vertices on sixty lines of
       the form: x1 y1   x2 y2   x3 y3

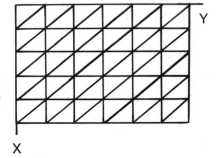

8. Roundoff Error and DOUBLE PRECISION

As we have seen, most applications of computers to calculus
involve the evaluation of several terms in a sequence. The
evaluations continue until some criterion is satisfied. In Figure 1-5
for example, the criterion was that the terms of two sequences differ
by less than 10^{-3}. In EXERCISE 5-5 the values of the sequence
$\dfrac{f(1.8 + 10^{-n}) - f(1.8)}{10^{-n}}$ was computed for some specific values of n,
namely, n = 1,2,3,4,5,6. In neither of these examples did we try to
compute the actual limit of the sequence involved. Indeed, as we
have noted in Section 6, limits cannot actually be computed because
arbitrary smallness cannot be achieved on a computer. Instead we
seek to use the computer to approximate the limit involved. As we
also remarked in Section 6, it is highly desirable to know that a
given sequence has a limit before we attempt to approximate it with
a computer. However, even when we know that a given sequence has a
limit, it may be difficult to approximate its value. In this Section
we discuss the problem and suggest both FORTRAN and mathematical
devices to reduce the problem.

In computations such as those referred to in the above examples,
there is more to the impossibility of achieving arbitrary smallness
than the maximum and minimum size of the numbers which the computer
can process. An even more important complication is the result of
roundoff. We were alluding to this, in Section 2, where we
commented briefly on difficulties caused by the restrictions on the
length and size of real numbers. That numbers are rounded, in the
computer, is the result of word length capability. Most numbers
(e.g., 1/3, 1/7, $\sqrt{2}$, π, etc.) require more decimal places for their
representation than is available in any computer. Most computers
operate in the binary or octal number systems. Fractions which have
finite length in the decimal system may have infinite length in the
binary and octal systems, systems commonly used in computers. For
example, .1(base 10)=.000110011001100...(base 2) and
.3(base 10)=.2314631463146...(base 8). (See EXERCISE 8-5). Thus,
most numbers generated in the computer are slightly in error. Errors
result from this is at least two distinct ways.

First, errors build up when we sum many approximate numbers.
In Figure 1-5 each term in a sequence is the result of many computations.
For the nth term in this sequence, these "many computations" result
from dividing the interval [2,5] into n subintervals, computing
$\log(x^2 + 5)$ at the left end of each of these subintervals and
multiplying each of these quantities by h. Finally, the nth term in
the sequence is the result of adding these n numbers[1]. Each of these
numbers is subject to rounding and, unfortunately, the roundoff errors
do not usually cancel out. Even if the average error is as small as
10^{-7}, it is easy to see what the effect of accumulating many roundoff
errors can be. If the sequence is the result of 5000 such computations,
it is clear the value in the third decimal place may be affected by
roundoff $(5 \times 10^3 \times 10^{-7} = 5 \times 10^{-4} = .0005)$. This effect is
illustrated in Figure 8-1 and in Figure 8-2. In Figure 8-1 the output
of EXERCISE 1-3 is given. In Figure 8-2 this output is repeated,
printing more decimal places and allowing the number of subdivisions
to become very large.

N	AREA	N	AREA
1	6.592	1	6.591674
2	7.568	2	7.567555
4	8.035	4	8.035470
8	8.265	8	8.265174
16	8.379	16	8.379026
32	8.436	32	8.435706
64	8.464	64	8.463985
128	8.478	128	8.478107
256	8.485	256	8.485163
512	8.489	512	8.488687
1024	8.490	1024	8.490440
2048	8.491	2048	8.491300
4096	8.492	4096	8.491699
		8192	8.491835
		16384	8.491775
		32768	8.491493
		65536	8.490844
		131072	8.489500
		262144	8.486832

Figure 8-1   Figure 8-2

It can be shown that the accuracy required in Figure 1-5 can be
achieved by using somewhat more than 4000 subdivisions of the interval
[2,5]. (See the discussion of error terms on page 10-105.) This
theoretical result can be seen (Figure 8-1) to agree with actual

---

[1] In Section 10 this term will be identified as a "lower sum".

computations. However, in some problems many more computations are required and then output such as in Figure 8-2 may result. In Figure 1-5, for example, due to roundoff error, an accuracy of 10^{-5} could not be obtained. This is partially due to the numerical methods used in that program. Later (Section 10 and Section 11) we shall discuss methods of overcoming the problem of accumulated roundoff error in discussion computerized solutions of two standard problems of calculus.

The other principal way[1] in which rounding generates errors is in differencing numbers of nearly the same size and adding numbers of greatly disparate size. Because of the limitation on the number of digits available in the representation of numbers, two numbers which have nearly the same value may have identical representations in the computer. Differencing of these numbers will, of course, produce a zero in the computer. An example of this phenomenon is furnished by computing values of the difference quotient in Problems 5-4 when the indicated processes are carried out for large values of n. The results are shown in Figure 8-3. After initially approaching the correct value 0.16, the values of the sequence begin

H	(F(X+H)-F(X))/H
1.00E-02	6.18000E-02
1.00E-04	1.59020E-01
1.00E-06	1.59990E-01
1.00E-08	1.60003E-01
1.00E-10	1.59730E-01
1.00E-12	1.70530E-01
1.00E-14	5.68434E+00
1.00E-16	0.

Figure 8-3

to fluctuate wildly. Such phenomena[2] can render computations meaningless and hence care must be exercised whenever the differencing of nearly equal numbers has an important effect on output. The reader is also referred to Rice and Rice[3] and an article by G. E. Forsythe[4].

---

[1] Other errors due to roundoff and the way the supplied functions are programmed may be present. The discussion of these is beyond the scope of these notes.

[2] Computer scientists refer to this as computational instability.

[3] ibid, pp. 314-318.

[4] Pitfalls in Computations, or Why a Math Book isn't enough, G. E. Forsythe, American Mathematical Monthly, November 1971.

We see, then, that differencing relatively large numbers with small inaccuracies can lead to computational difficulties as readily as can summing many numbers with small inaccuracies. Methods of avoiding these errors are part of the subject of more advanced courses usually named "Numerical Analysis." In Section 10 and Section 11, we introduce some elementary techniques for numerical integration which greatly reduce the number of additions required in problems such as that programmed in Figure 1-5.

We have seen that because only a finite number of places is available for the approximate representation of numbers, roundoff errors are routinely generated in computers. In some types of numerical procedures it is not uncommon for 10,000 additions of numbers suffering such defects to occur. If, because of the limitations of the machine, only 7 decimal places are available, it is clear that only 3 of them can be relied on. This degree of accuracy may be incompatible with the needs of the user.

Three partial remedies are available. The first is to use a computer with more space allotted to the representation of real numbers. Naturally, this may be impossible for a number of reasons. However, for the effect of such representations, compare Figures 8-1, 2 which were generated on an IBM 7094 with Figure 8-4 which is the corresponding table generated on a CDC 6500.

The second and more reasonable solution is to use the DOUBLE PRECISION feature of FORTRAN. The actual number of spaces allowed for numbers of digits in a DOUBLE PRECISION quantity is sometimes more than double that in a single-precision number. It is safe to assume that DOUBLE PRECISION increases the number of digits by about 75%. Figure 8-5 gives the result of running Figure 1-5 in DOUBLE PRECISION on the IBM 7094. The results are indistinguishable from those of Figure 8-4 where are reported the results of running that program on the CDC 6500.

The third remedy for these problems is to use more refined numerical techniques. Most of these are beyond the scope of this course and, as we have remarked, are included in courses in Numerical Analysis. Some elementary methods of this type will be introduced in Section 10 and Section 12.

	SINGLE PRECISION RUN OF EXERCISE 1-3 ON THE CDC 6500			DOUBLE PRECISION RUN OF EXERCISE 1-3 ON THE IBM 7094
1	6.591674		1	6.591674
2	7.567555		2	7.567555
4	8.035471		4	8.035471
8	8.265174		8	8.265174
16	8.379026		16	8.379026
32	8.435707		32	8.435707
64	8.463986		64	8.463986
128	8.478110		128	8.478110
256	8.485169		256	8.485169
512	8.488697		512	8.488697
1024	8.490461		1024	8.490461
2048	8.491343		2048	8.491343
4096	8.491784		4096	8.491784
8192	8.492004		8192	8.492004
16384	8.492114		16384	8.492114
32768	8.492169		32768	8.492169
65536	8.492197		65536	8.492197
131072	8.492211		131072	8.492211
262144	8.492218		262144	8.492218

Figure 8-4   Figure 8-5

We devote a few lines to a possible remedy in the case of differencing disparately size numbers. Here it is occasionally possible to perform an algebraic rearrangement of terms before submitting the problem to the computer. For example, Figure 8-6 gives a program for computing $(1 + x - 1)/x$ by various uses of the associative law and by DOUBLE PRECISION variables. Although the expression is identically equal to one for all x, the values of the expression are quite different from this except when DOUBLE PRECISION is used. While this is a strong argument for the use of DOUBLE PRECISION, it is an even stronger argument for doing all that is possible to simplify expressions before committing them to the machine. DOUBLE PRECISION is expensive in terms of machine time and merely delays the onset of the effect of roundoff error.

Variables have their value computed in DOUBLE PRECISION by declaring them to be of this type at the beginning of the program. A statement of the form

DOUBLE PRECISION NAME1,NAME2,···,NAMEn

is used. As DOUBLE PRECISION applies only to real numbers, it is unnecessary to declare variables beginning with I,J,K,L,M or N REAL if they are also declared to be DOUBLE PRECISION.

```
      DOUBLE PRECISION DX,DF,DY
      F(X)=((1.+X)-1.)/X
      G(X)=(1.+(X-1.))/X
      DF(DX)=((1.D0+DX)-1.D0)/DX
      PRINT 10
   10 FORMAT(13X,'X',12X,'F(X)',10X,'G(X)',9X,'DF(X)',9X,'Z'/)
      X=1.E-7
      DX=1.D-7
   12 Y=F(X)
      W=G(X)
      DY=DF(DX)
      Z=DY
      PRINT 11,X,Y,W,DY,Z
   11 FORMAT(5X,3E14.5,D14.5,F10.5)
      IF(X.LT.2.E-23)STOP
      X=X/3.
      DX=DX/3.D0
      GO TO 12
      END
```

X	F(X)	G(X)	DF(X)	Z
1.00000E-07	1.00000E+00	1.00000E+00	1.00000D+00	1.00000
3.33333E-08	1.00000E+00	1.00000E+00	1.00000D+00	1.00000
1.11111E-08	9.99999E-01	1.00000E+00	1.00000D+00	1.00000
3.70370E-09	9.99998E-01	1.00000E+00	1.00000D+00	1.00000
1.23457E-09	9.99994E-01	1.00000E+00	1.00000D+00	1.00000
4.11523E-10	9.99989E-01	1.00001E+00	1.00000D+00	1.00000
1.37174E-10	9.99971E-01	1.00002E+00	1.00000D+00	1.00000
4.57247E-11	9.99971E-01	1.00013E+00	1.00000D+00	1.00000
1.52416E-11	9.99971E-01	1.00044E+00	1.00000D+00	1.00000
5.08053E-12	9.99971E-01	1.00137E+00	1.00000D+00	1.00000
1.69351E-12	9.98573E-01	1.00277E+00	1.00000D+00	1.00000
5.64503E-13	9.94377E-01	1.00696E+00	1.00000D+00	1.00000
1.88168E-13	9.81790E-01	1.01955E+00	1.00000D+00	1.00000
6.27225E-14	9.06268E-01	1.01955E+00	1.00000D+00	1.00000
2.09075E-14	6.79701E-01	1.01955E+00	1.00000D+00	1.00000
6.96917E-15	0	1.01955E+00	1.00000D+00	1.00000
2.32306E-15	0	3.05865E+00	1.00000D+00	1.00000
7.74352E-16	0	9.17596E+00	1.00000D+00	1.00000
2.58117E-16	0	2.75279E+01	1.00000D+00	1.00000
8.60392E-17	0	8.25836E+01	1.00000D+00	1.00000
2.86797E-17	0	2.47751E+02	1.00000D+00	1.00000
9.55991E-18	0	7.43253E+02	1.00000D+00	1.00000
3.18664E-18	0	2.22976E+03	1.00000D+00	1.00000
1.06221E-18	0	6.68928E+03	1.00000D+00	1.00000
3.54071E-19	0	2.00678E+04	1.00000D+00	1.00000
1.18024E-19	0	6.02035E+04	1.00000D+00	1.00000
3.93412E-20	0	1.80610E+05	1.00000D+00	1.00000
1.31137E-20	0	5.41831E+05	1.00000D+00	1.00000
4.37124E-21	0	1.62549E+06	1.00000D+00	1.00000
1.45708E-21	0	4.87648E+06	1.00000D+00	1.00000
4.85694E-22	0	1.46294E+07	1.00000D+00	1.00000
1.61898E-22	0	4.38883E+07	1.00000D+00	1.00000
5.39660E-23	0	1.31665E+08	1.00000D+00	1.00000
1.79887E-23	0	3.94995E+08	9.99999D-01	1.00000

Figure 8-6

DOUBLE PRECISION quantities are combined with others arithmetically by all the rules previously studied for ordinary reals and by the same symbols. DOUBLE PRECISION quantities may be combined arithmetically with ordinary reals. The operations are performed in DOUBLE PRECISION and stored that way if the variable on the left has been declared to be of this type. Of course, rounding errors already present in the single precision real will be present in the DOUBLE PRECISION result.

Simple constants may also be introduced in single precision even when they are to be combined with DOUBLE PRECISION constants and variables. However, to avoid the introduction of roundoff errors, in even these simple cases, it is preferable to use DOUBLE PRECISION constants when DOUBLE PRECISION values are desired.

DOUBLE PRECISION notation for constants is of exponential type but using a D in place of E. 2.6D3, 1.D-2, 7.167432658916D2, etc. are examples of DOUBLE PRECISION constants.

The values of DOUBLE PRECISION variables are output with the field descriptor Dm.n. The basic rules are the same as for E descriptors except that more digits may be called for. F and E field descriptors should not be used to output DOUBLE PRECISION variables.

DOUBLE PRECISION functions are also supplied. ALOG becomes DLOG and ALOG10 becomes DLOG10. All other real valued functions listed in Table 4.1 convert by prefixing D. Thus, DEXP is the DOUBLE PRECISION version of the exponential function. DOUBLE PRECISION functions require DOUBLE PRECISION arguments and vice versa.

EXERCISES

8-1   Rewrite EXERCISE 5-4 in DOUBLE PRECISION. Run and compare with Figure 8-3. What do you observe?

8-2   The area of a circle may be approximated by generating sequences of n inscribed and circumscribed rectangle as in the sketch. Write both SINGLE and DOUBLE PRECISION programs to approximate the area of the unit circle to within 10^{-5}. Start with n = 1 and double n on each succeeding approximation. Also stop if n exceeds 10^5.

8-3   (a)   Let θ be the central angle of a circular sector and A_1 the area of the inscribed polygon as indicated in Figure 1. Let A_2 be the area of the inscribed polygon shown in Figure 2. Show that $A_2 = A_1 \sec(\theta/2)$. In general, show that $A_{n+1} = A_n \sec(\theta/2^n)$. Similarly, show for the circumscribed polygons, as in Figure 3, that $A_{n+1} = A_n (2 \tan(\theta/2^n))/\tan(\theta/2^{n-1})$.

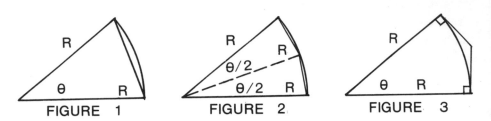

FIGURE 1   FIGURE 2   FIGURE 3

(b)   For the unit circle, inscribe and circumscribe regular polygons of n sides.   The area of the circle ($= \pi$) is between these two polygonal areas.   Starting with six sides, successively double the number of sides of the polygons until the difference between the areas of the inscribed and circumscribed polygons differ by less than 5×10^{-6} and thus approximate π to five decimal places.   Stop if the number of inscribed triangles exceeds 10^5.

8-4   Rerun EXERCISE 6-5 in DOUBLE PRECISION.

8-5   Rewrite the program for EXERCISE 3-4 so that k is determined automatically.   Use this program to find $\sqrt{1.23}$, $\sqrt{4.3256}$ and $\sqrt{52.46091}$.   Machine representation of numbers can cause problems.

8-6   Rewrite the above program so that P decimal places are determined when $P \geq k$ and k decimal places are determined if $k > P$.   Run the program for the roots in EXERCISE 8-5 for P = 3.

8-7   In base b, $0.a_1a_2a_3\ldots$ means $\dfrac{a_1}{b} + \dfrac{a_2}{b^2} + \dfrac{a_3}{b^3} + \cdots$.   Write a program to convert decimal fractions to an arbitrary base $b > 1$. Use it to find 10 places in the binary representation of .1 and .3 (both base 10).

9. A Potpourri of FORTRAN Statements.

Those portions of FORTRAN which we have already considered enable us to meet most of the programming requirements of calculus. In the present section we discuss briefly some additional FORTRAN capabilities which round out an introduction to FORTRAN. The various statements which follow are discussed independently wherever possible. The order of presentation does not imply a hierarchy of importance among the statements.

9A. DO.

The DO statement (DO loop) provides an alternative to loops involving the use of the logical IF. It can be used for exitting from loops in those cases where a set of operations is to be performed a specified number of times as well as when some specified condition is satisfied.

The form is:

   DO J I = K,M,N

In the DO STATEMENT, J is a statement number, I is an integer variable and K,M,N are integer variables which previously have been assigned positive values or they are positive integer constants. I,K,M,N are called <u>indices</u>. This statement causes the block of statements (called the <u>range</u> of the DO statement) starting with the one immediately after the DO and ending with one numbered J to be executed once each for I = K, I = K + N, I = K + 2N,··· so long as I does not exceed M,[1] unless within the DO loop control was transferred to some other part of the program. If the prescribed circuits of the loop are completed without control being transferred to some other part of the program, control passes to the statement after the one numbered J. No variable among I, K, M, N can appear on the left side of an assignment statement, that is, none can have its value changed by an assignment statement in the DO loop where it is an index.

In many cases N is equal to 1. Then the DO is written:

   DO J I = K,M

---
[1]That is, the range is executed [1 + (M - K)/N] times.

Although anything which can be done by a DO statement can also be done with the logical IF, many programmers feel that the DO is easier to use. However, there are some restrictions on its use. In many versions of FORTRAN the first and last statement in the range of a DO must be executable statements.[1] Also, in many versions the last statement may not transfer control to a statement outside the range of the DO. We shall avoid these problems through the use of CONTINUE which is discussed below. Transfer of control into the range of a DO is also prohibited although control may be transferred to the DO itself. Transfer out of the DO loop from an interior statement is permissible. A special "executable" statement is provided for use when the last statement in the DO would otherwise violate the above rules. It is:

CONTINUE

Other than marking the end of the range of a DO loop, CONTINUE has no effect. For beginning programmers, it is not unreasonable to end all DO loops with CONTINUE.

Task: Compute and print to 3 decimal places the value of $\displaystyle\sum_{k=1}^{n} \frac{1}{1 + k^2}$

for n = 1,2,$\cdots$ 50.

Program:

```
      SUM=0.²
      DO 1 N=1,50
      SUM=SUM + 1./(1.+(FLOAT(N))**2)
      PRINT 2,N,SUM
    2 FORMAT(I3,F15.3)
    1 CONTINUE
      END
```

An alternate to the use of CONTINUE would have been to number the PRINT statement 1. FORMAT, being nonexecutable could not have been the last statement in the range.

In some cases it is necessary to nest DO's. These cases are characterized by the necessity to perform repeatedly a block of statements in which each performance of the block requires the repeated

---

[1] The only nonexecutable statements which we have encountered are type statements, END, FORMAT statements and statement functions.

[2] In some systems, the initiallizing statement SUM=0. is not required. However, such initializations are recommended as good general programming practice.

performance of a sub-block. DO loops cannot overlap or share indices.
An example is provided by rephrasing Figure 1-5 in terms of DO's.

Looked at in terms of repetitions of blocks of instructions,
Figure 1-5 asks the repeated calculation of $\sum\limits_{k=1}^{N} f(x + kH)\cdot H$ for
several values of N until the quantity $[\log(F(B)) - \log(F(A))]\cdot H$
becomes sufficiently small. In the next example we use a nest of two
loops to accomplish this. We also make other minor modifications in
the original program to improve the efficiency of the computation.
Some of the intuitive nature of the original program is lost thereby.

Task: Rewrite the program in Figure 1-5 using DO loops as described
above.

Program:

```
C   THIS PROGRAM APPROXIMATES THE AREA UNDER THE CURVE F(X)=LOG(X**2+5)
C   BETWEEN X=A AND X=B TO WITHIN .001 SQUARE UNITS.  THE AREA IS
C   APPROXIMATED BY THE SUM OF AREAS OF INSCRIBED RECTANGLES:
C   INTL=F(A)*H+F(A+H)*H+...+F(A+N*H)*H WHERE N=(B-A)/N. COMPUTATION
C   OF INTL IS PERFORMED FOR N=2,4,8,...2**M FOR ALL M BETWEEN 1 AND
C   25 UNLESS TERMINATED EARLIER BY THE DIFFERENCE (F(B) - F(A))*H
C   BECOMING SMALLER THAN .001.
        REAL INTL
        F(X)=ALOG(X*X+5)
        A=2.
        B=5.
        E=.001
        QUIT=F(B)-F(A)
        PRINT 1
      1 FORMAT(1X,... as in FIGURE 1-5...)
        H=B-A
        DO 4 M=1,25
C   CALCULATE NEW H TO GO WITH THIS M.
        H=H/2
        IF(QUIT*H.LT.E)STOP
C   CALCULATE INTL FOR N=2**M.
        INTL=0
        X=A
        N=2**M
        DO 2 J=1,N
        INTL=INTL+F(X)*H
        X=X+H
      2 CONTINUE
        PRINT 3,N,INT
      3 FORMAT(14X,I8,30X,F7.3)
      4 CONTINUE
        END
```

In this example the <u>inner</u> DO is just the four statements

```
        DO 2 J=1,N
        INT=INT+ALOG(F(X))*H
        X+H
      2 CONTINUE
```

In this loop N is an integer variable which has been given a positive value (2^M) in the <u>outer</u> DO. Although N does appear on the left of an assignment statement, this appearance is not in the DO loop in which it is an index. In the outer DO a CONTINUE is needed because the logical IF transfers control outside the DO loop.

9B.　Subscripted variables and the DIMENSION statement.

In ordinary mathematical notation, subscripts provide a powerful tool for denoting, sequentially, large arrays of numbers. For example, $\{a_i\}$, i = 1,2,... may denote all the elements of a sequence. Such arrays are sometimes referred to as "one-dimensional." They may, of course, contain only finitely many elements. Arrays may also be "two-dimensional" as in the determinant $|a_{ij}|$, i, j = 1,2,...,n. Not all two-dimensional arrays need be "square" as examples in this section will show.

In FORTRAN, subscripts as written above do not exist. Instead of a_i, one writes A(I); instead of a_{ij}, one writes A(I,J). A(I), A(I,J) are called subscripted variables. They provide the same economy of symbols in FORTRAN as in ordinary mathematical notation. That is, a single symbol, with subscripts, may represent several values of a variable or several variables, one for each value of the subscript.

Upon appropriate instructions from the programmer, the compiler sets aside storage locations sufficient in number to receive all the values in the array. The statement which does this is DIMENSION. All subscripted variables must appear in a DIMENSION statement. If a subscripted variable T will have 635 values in a program the compiler is so instructed by the statement:

　　DIMENSION T(635)

If the programmer is uncertain as to the number of values which T will have, an upper bound on this number should be used. No harm will usually be done by being generous in estimating the number of values to be stored. Underestimating the number of values to be stored will result in execution being terminated short of completion of the program.

A two-dimensional array W of "13 rows" and "25 columns" would be provided for by the statement:

　　DIMENSION W(13,25)

Were these to appear in the same program the statement:

　　DIMENSION W(13,25),T(635)

would alert the compiler to set aside the necessary 635+(13×25)=960 locations.

Subscripted variables obey the same naming conventions as other variables. Naturally, all of the variables in an array must be of the same type. The subscripts themselves must be either integer constants or integer variables. No subscript can have a value less than 1. In addition subscripts may be computed as sums, differences or products of integer constants or integer variables but no other form of computation is permitted. Thus, NAME*LAKE is a permissible subscript but NAME**2 is not.

Associated with subscripted variables is the concept of the implied DO loop. Implied DO loops allow the programmer to output subscripted variables without listing each one separately, or in a chain, in a PRINT statement. Several examples will illustrate.

a) Suppose ITEM(1), ITEM(2), ... , ITEM(100) are stored in the computer. To output all of them we write

   PRINT k,(ITEM(J),J=1,100)

b) To output only those for even J we write

   PRINT k,(ITEM(J),J=2,100,2)

c) To output ITEM(6), ITEM(7), ... , ITEM(10) we write

   PRINT k,(ITEM(J),J=6,10)

   or

   PRINT k,ITEM(6),ITEM(7),ITEM(8),ITEM(9),ITEM(10)

Obviously, the number of values of ITEM which can be printed on one line depends upon the number of spaces required for each value and the spacing between them. These factors influence the associated FORMAT statement.

   k FORMAT(1X,rIp)

outputs r values of ITEM per line, each right justified in p printing spaces. rp must not exceed the capability of the printer being used.

d) Suppose that the 10×20 integer array A is stored in the computer That is, suppose that the values of A(1,1), A(1,2), ... , A(1,20), ... , A(10,20) are stored. To output the array we write

   PRINT k,((A(I,J),J=1,20),I=1,10)
   k FORMAT(1X,20Ip)

e) Of course, 20p should not exceed the number of printing spaces available. If this limit will be exceeded, the array can be output in two (or more) segments such as

```
   PRINT k,((A(I,J),J=1,10),I=1,10)
   PRINT k,((A(I,J),J=11,20),I=1,10)
k FORMAT(1X,10Ip)
```

f) The array which has the columns of A as rows and vice versa is called the _transpose_ of A. It is output by

```
   PRINT k,((A(I,J),I=1,10),J=1,20)
k FORMAT(1X,10Ip)
```

g) If the one dimensional array B has as many elements as the rows of A (i.e., I elements) then the _augmented_ array A,B with B as rightmost column is output by

```
   PRINT k,((A(I,J),J=1,20)B(I),I=1,10)
k FORMAT(1X,21Ip)
```

h) Selected values of an array can be printed by calling for them by name. For example, to output the fifth row of A and the element A(6,15) we write

```
   PRINT k,(A(5,M),M=1,20),A(6,15)
k FORMAT(1x,21Ip)
```

   Figure 9-1 illustrates the use of subscripted variables.

9C. The READ statement. The data deck.

   So far all of the numbers which we have used in our program have been introduced as simple constants or via assignment statements in a program. Occasionally, the programmer will be called upon to solve problems which call for the same program to be run several times for different sets of parameters. For example, it may be required to approximate the roots of several polynomials: the coefficients would be the parameters; it may be required to average the grades of a class: the grades of each student are the parameters; etc.

   While it would be possible to copy the source deck - once for each set of parameters - this is clearly not an elegant way to handle the problem. The FORTRAN statement READ[1] provides the desired capability. The READ statement instructs the computer to read the parameter values from a special deck.

---

[1] The Standards Institute requires at least READ (n,k) where n refers to the unit from which the data is to be read. The card reader is usually unit 5.

```
      DIMENSION NTLOG(100),C(100)
      REAL INT,NTLOG
      I=1
      A=1.
      B=1.
      PRINT 100
100 FORMAT('1',20X,'SHORT TABLE OF NATURAL LOGARITHMS'//'  N',5X,'0',6
   1X,'1',6X,'2',6X,'3',6X,'4',6X,'5',6X,'6',6X,'7',6X,'8',6X,'9'//)
  4 H=(B-A)/100.
      RN=1.
      INT=1./A+1./B
  2 INT=INT+2./(A+RN*H)
      RN=RN+1.
      IF(RN.GT.99.)GO TO 1
      GO TO 2
  1 NTLOG(I)=INT*H/2.
      I=I+1
      B=B+.1
      IF(I.GT.100)GO TO 3
      GO TO 4
  3 K=1
  6 M=K+9
      C(K)=FLOAT(K/10+1)
      PRINT 5,C(K),(NTLOG(J),J=K,M)
  5 FORMAT(1X,F3.0,10F7.3)
      K=K+10
      IF(K.GT.95)STOP
      GO TO 6
      END
```

Figure 9-1

SHORT TABLE OF NATURAL LOGARITHMS

N	0	1	2	3	4	5	6	7	8	9
1.	0.	0.095	0.182	0.262	0.336	0.405	0.470	0.531	0.588	0.642
2.	0.693	0.742	0.788	0.833	0.875	0.916	0.956	0.993	1.030	1.065
3.	1.099	1.131	1.163	1.194	1.224	1.253	1.281	1.308	1.335	1.361
4.	1.386	1.411	1.435	1.459	1.482	1.504	1.526	1.548	1.569	1.589
5.	1.610	1.629	1.649	1.668	1.687	1.705	1.723	1.741	1.758	1.775
6.	1.792	1.808	1.825	1.841	1.857	1.872	1.887	1.902	1.917	1.932
7.	1.946	1.960	1.974	1.988	2.002	2.015	2.029	2.042	2.055	2.067
8.	2.080	2.092	2.105	2.117	2.129	2.141	2.152	2.164	2.175	2.187
9.	2.198	2.209	2.220	2.231	2.241	2.252	2.262	2.273	2.283	2.293
10.	2.303	2.313	2.323	2.333	2.343	2.352	2.362	2.371	2.380	2.390

Figure 9-2

From our previous work with output formatting, we expect that some code will be required to specify the types of numbers being read and their locations on the cards of the data deck. Type is indicated in READ as in PRINT FORMATS by I,F,E and D. As in PRINT, the widths of field in a READ statement are cumulative. Thus, the specifications I6,F14.6,F10.2 indicate an integer, right justified in the first 6 columns of a data card, followed by one real in columns 7 through 20 and one real in columns 21 through 30. It is not necessary to punch the decimal point in a real number. However, if a decimal point is punched and is in a different location from that given in the F,E or D specification, the decimal point actually punched will take precedence over the indicated one. Data separation from the main program is shown in Figure 9-3.

Figure 9-3 illustrates data decks and the above decimal point options. Both programs input the same data and output the same results.

SOURCE decks followed by DATA decks:

```
3 READ 1,A,B,C,N                    3 READ 1,A,B,C,N
1 FORMAT(3F2.0,I1)                  1 FORMAT(3F3.0,I1)
  S=(A+B+C)/3                         S=(A+B+C)/3
  PRINT 2,A,B,C,S                     PRINT 2,A,B,C,S
2 FORMAT(1X,4F6.1)                  2 FORMAT(1X,4F6.1)
  IF(N.EQ.0)GO TO 3                   IF(N.EQ.0)GO TO 3
  END                                 END
7/8/9                               7/8/9
616283                              61.62.83.
704267                              70.42.67.
9091921                             90.91.92.1
```

Output of above programs:
```
61.0    62.0    83.0    68.7
70.0    42.0    67.0    59.7
90.0    91.0    92.0    91.0
```

Figure 9-3

In Figure 9-3, special attention is called to the integer N in the READ statement and the numeral punched in column 7. It is sometimes called the monitor and signals the end of the deck. Since it is used only for this purpose, it is convenient to use a nonzero integer so that nothing need be punched in the other cards of the data deck.

In the program in Figure 9-3 each triple of numbers A,B,C is read in and processed before the next is read. Sometimes, however, it is useful to read an entire data deck into the computer before processing any of the data. If all the data are on one card (i.e., qm + rp < 80) this is accomplished by

```
      READ 4,REAL,MINK¹
   4 FORMAT(qFm.n,rIp)
```

If one value of REAL and one of MINK is on each of M cards, use

```
      DO 1 J=1,M
      READ 2,REAL(J),MINK(J)
   2 FORMAT(Fm.n,Ip)
   1 CONTINUE
```

All numbers punched in the data deck must be right-justified in the columns specified by the associated field descriptor.

In data cards blanks are read as zeros. For example, with the field descriptor I6, 6∼∼∼∼∼ is stored as 600000, ∼∼6∼∼∼ is stored as 6000 and ∼∼∼∼∼6 is stored as 6.

9D.   Subprograms.

In EXERCISE 5-3 we were called upon to compute the values of a rather complicated function and then approximate its maximum value. In EXERCISE 5-4 we were asked for these values and then were also asked to evaluate the difference quotient $(F(X+H) - F(X))/H$ at the X at which F achieved its maximum (approximately). The results were rather complicated programs.

One way to avoid such complicated programs is to write them in segments which can be linked by GO TO's. For example, EXERCISE 5-3 could be broken into the segments: (a) Evaluate $F(X)$ and (b) Find its maximum value. Flow charts might have the appearance of Figure 9-4 where the value of $F(X)$ in the main program at the right is to be supplied by the program segment at the left. FORTRAN programs to accomplish this linking are given in Figure 9-5. The segment may be inserted in its entirety place of both GO TO 100. In writing this main program and segment, it was necessary to avoid using in either part a statement number already used in the other and also to be certain that variables shared between the two had the same names. Obviously, this could be quite burdensome if there were several longer segments to be integrated into one main program. The sub-program capability of FORTRAN eases these difficulties.

---

[1]Of course, this calls for an appropriate DIMENSION statement.

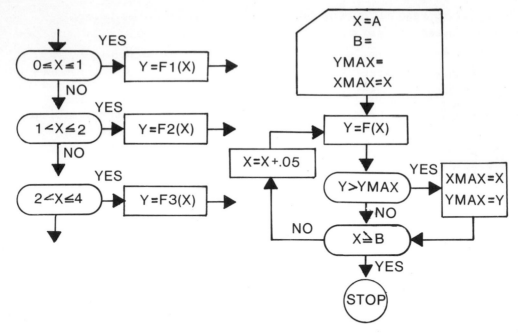

Figure 9-4

Segment (for evaluating f(x)):

```
100 IF(X.GE.0..AND.X.LE.1.)GO TO 101
    IF(X.GT.1..AND.X.LE.2.)GO TO 102
    IF(X.GT.2..AND.X.LE.4.)GO TO 103
101 Y=X*(8.-X**2)
    GO TO 1
102 Y=(2.*X-1.)*(8.-X**2)
    GO TO 1
103 Y=(2.*X-1.)*4./(X-1.)
    GO TO 1
```

Main Program:

```
    X=
    B=
    YMAX=
    XMAX=X
    GO TO 100
  1 IF(Y.LE.YMAX)GO TO 2
    YMAX=Y
    XMAX=X
  2 IF(X.GE.B)GO TO 3
    X=X+.05
    GO TO 100
  3 PRINT 4,XMAX,YMAX
  4 FORMAT(2F10.2)
    (...segment could be inserted here...)
    END
```

Figure 9-5

There are two types of subprograms: (1) FUNCTION subprograms and (2) SUBROUTINE subprograms. The example given above can be further simplified through the use of the FUNCTION subprogram. We discuss it first, then turn to SUBROUTINES.

The FUNCTION subprogram is named FUNCTION followed by the name which the function has in the main program. It contains the statements necessary to evaluate the function and one or more RETURNs to return computation to the main program as appropriate. The main program and subprograms used with it have their own END cards. The form is

```
FUNCTION NAME(ARG1,ARG2,···,ARGN)
   ⋮
NAME=
   ⋮
RETURN
   ⋮
END
```

As in statement functions, the arguments ARG1, ARG2,..., ARGN are dummy variables used in the subprogram to evaluate NAME. When the subprogram is called for in the main program, the function NAME, evaluated at arguments known in the main program, is used as a variable just as in the case of statement functions. Internally, these argument values are transferred to the subprogram for execution by the subprogram. Naturally, the order of the arguments has the same significance as in mathematics, i.e., the variables must be in the same order in both the main program and the FUNCTION subprogram.

Figure 9-6 gives the main program and a FUNCTION subprogram for Problem 5-3.

```
                                 FUNCTION F(X)
    X=0.                         IF(X.GE.0..AND.X.LE.1.)GO TO 1
    B=4.                         IF(X.GT.1..AND.X.LE.2.)GO TO 2
    YMAX=0.                      IF(X.GT.2..AND.X.LE.4.)GO TO 3
    XMAX=X                     1 F=X*(8.-X**2)
  2 Y=F(X)                       RETURN
    IF(Y.LE.YMAX)GO TO 1       2 F=(2.*X-1.)*(8.-X**2)
    YMAX=Y                       RETURN
    XMAX=X                     3 F=(2.*X-1.)*4./(X-1.)
  1 IF(X.GE.B)GO TO 3            RETURN
    X=X+.05                      END
    GO TO 2
  3 PRINT 4,XMAX,YMAX
  4 FORMAT(2F10.2)
    END
```

Figure 9-6

The complete job consists of the main program followed by one or more FUNCTION subprograms.

Not only can the main program call on more than one FUNCTION subprogram, but one such subprogram can call on another. However, two subprograms may not call on each other. If the name of the function in a FUNCTION subprogram is to be declared of type different than dictated by the naming conventions the type statement preceeds the FUNCTION statement. For example, if INT(X) is to be real valued and DOUBLE PRECISION, the subprogram would be entitled

    DOUBLE PRECISION FUNCTION INT(X)

Functions defined this way may have many arguments. Even arrays themselves may be included among the arguments but the further development of this point is beyond the scope of this book.

Whereas a FUNCTION subprogram outputs to the main program a single value, the value of the function, a SUBROUTINE may output several values. These values may be of mixed type. Thus, the name of a SUBROUTINE has no type associated with it. However, the names of the values output must follow the usual rules. The form of the SUBROUTINE subprogram is:

    SUBROUTINE NAME(ARG1,ARG2,···,ARGN)
        .
        .
        .

    RETURN
    END

Within the subprogram some of the arguments are specified by values passed from the main program (by a technique to be discussed shortly) and the others are computed in the subroutine. As we have indicated, not all of the arguments need be of the same type. Since the name of a SUBROUTINE has no value associated with it (as a FUNCTION has) a device must exist for introducing its values into the main program. The device is the statement CALL. The form, as part of the main program, is

        .
        .
        .

    CALL NAME(ARGU1,ARGU2,···,ARGUN)
        .
        .
        .

    END

The list ARGU1,···,ARGUN need not be the same list of variables and constants as ARG1,ARG2,···,ARGN but the lists must be of the same length and types must be in the same order. NAME must be the same in both the main program and the subprogram.

When NAME is called by the main program, the values of, say, ARGU1,···,ARGUK are transferred to the subprogram as the values of ARG1,ARG2,···,ARGK in that order. (Actually, the remaining set ARGK+1,···,ARGUN is transferred too, but a discussion of this fact requires a deeper examination of the action of the compiler then we wish to undertake. Since the remaining set have not been assigned any values, no violence is done by ignoring them in the description of this action.) The remaining set is then assigned values in the subprogram and returned to the main program. An example of a subroutine is given in Figure 9-7.

```
        A=1.
        B=2.                          SUBROUTINE SMORG(X,Y,Z,U,V,W)
        C=3.                          U=X+Y
        D=4.                          V=Y+Z
        E=5.                          W=X+Y+Z
        F=6.                          RETURN
        CALL SMORG(A,B,C,D,E,F)       END
        PRINT 1,D,E,F
      1 FORMAT(3F10.2)
        END
```

Figure 9-7

The output of this program is

    3.00   5.00   6.00

Neither function subprograms nor subroutines should be given the name of a supplied function.

In addition to supplied and arithmetic functions (Section 4) and the function subprograms and subroutines discussed here, most Computer Centers maintain a "library" of special purpose subroutines. These include programs to generate random numbers, analyze statistical data, plot points, do numerical integrations and find roots and many others. The reader should consult the Center Library.

9E.   Alphameric Constants.[1]

We have seen that the FORTRAN Hollerith descriptor provides for printing table and column heading which allow for aesthetically pleasing

---

[1]Not available in SBF.

output.   In programs such as that for EXERCISE 7-4, it would be nice
to be able to output alphabetic symbols which vary with the pass
through the loop, the magnitude of some quantity, etc.   This can be
done through the use of the <u>alphameric</u> field descriptor.   This
descriptor allows the programmer to assign to <u>integer</u> variables
"constant" values which are merely collections of symbols from the
available character set.   The maximum number of symbols which may be
used in such a constant varies with the computer.

The alphameric descriptor has the form Ap, where p is the field
width.   The assignment described above is accomplished through the use
of READ.   (The DATA statement, which we do not discuss here, may also
be used.)   For example,

```
    INTEGER BLANK,DOT,X
    READ(5,1)BLANK,DOT,X
  1 FORMAT(3A1)
```

with a data card such as Figure 9-8, assigns to the integer variables
BLANK, DOT X respectively, the values ~,.,X.   These "values" may be
transferred to other integer variables just as any other values may.

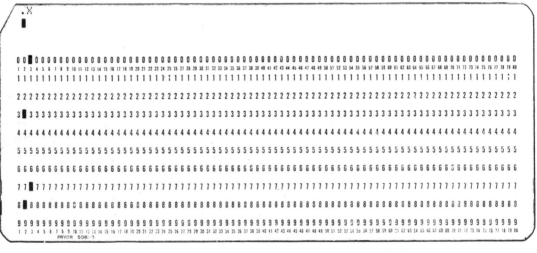

Figure 9-8

Figure 9-9 gives a simple program illustrating this concept and
Figure 9-10 gives a more complicated program.   Studying Figure 9-10
is also instructive in that it illustrates many of the other concepts
discussed in this section.

On output, alphameric symbols use the same descriptor, Ap.

While the length of an alphameric constant may not exceed six
characters, p may be larger.   The justification of alphameric constants

is somewhat different from that for numbers. Numbers are always right-justified in their fields. This is not the case with alphameric constants.

Suppose that q characters is the maximum number of spaces available for alphameric constants. On input, if $p > q$; that is, if more spaces are delineated on the data card than are allowed for such constants, the q right-most symbols will be read. On the other hand, if $p \leq q$; that is, if the alphameric constant is within the imposed size limitation, the input constant is read into the left-most of the allowed q spaces with $q - p$ trailing blanks if $p < q$.

On output, if $p > q$; that is, if more printing spaces are allowed than the maximum (not necessarily the actual) size of the alphameric constant, the output will have the form of $p - q$ blanks followed by the constant and, if the constant is shorter than q, followed by blanks. If $p \leq q$, the output will be that part (possibly all) of the alphameric constant stored in the p left-most spaces.

The effect of these rather complicated rules can be minimized by limiting the size of alphameric constants to that allowed by the computer and using exactly the size of the constant in the field descriptor on both input and output. Spacing requirements should be met through appropriate use of the Hollerith or the skip descriptors.

```
      INTEGER BLANK,DOT,X
      READ(5.1) BLANK,DOT,X
    1 FORMAT(3A1)
      K=1
      ITEM=BLANK
      JTEM=DOT
      KTEM=X
    3 IF(K.EQ.1)PRINT 2,ITEM
      IF(K.EQ.2)PRINT 2,JTEM
      IF(K.EQ.3)PRINT 2,KTEM
      IF(K.GE.3)STOP
      K=K+1
      GO TO 3
    2 FORMAT(1X,'SYMBOL IS',A10/)
      END

**0**      EXECUTION


SYMBOL IS

SYMBOL IS    .

SYMBOL IS    X
```

Figure 9-9

```
C1    PROGRAM PLOTS POINTS ON GRAPH SYMMETRIC ABOUT X-AXIS.  FOR FUNCTIONS REMOVE
C     REFERENCE TO TO J2.  DOMAIN OF RELATION OR FUNCTION MUST HAVE LENGTH 14 OR
C     LESS.  Y MAY VARY FROM -8 TO +8.  X-AXIS IS MIDPOINT OF LINE.  7 PRINTING
C     POSITIONS IN LINE IS 1 Y-UNIT, 4 PRINTING LINES IS 1 X-UNIT.
      DIMENSION LINE (121)
C2    BLANK INITIALIZES PRINTING POSITIONS, DOT PRINTS AXES, ONE AND TWO MARK
C     POSITIVE UNITS ON THE AXES, STAR DENOTES OTHER UNIT VALUES, OH THE ORIGIN
C     AND X PLOTTED POINTS.  NEXT 3 LINES DEFINE FUNCTION TO BE PLOTTED AND GIVE
C     LIMITS ON ITS DOMAIN. THESE MAY NOT DIFFER BY MORE THAN 14.
      INTEGER BLANK,DOT,X,ONE,TWO,STAR,OH
      Y(Z)=(8./7.)*SQRT(49.-Z*Z)
      A=-7.
      B=7.
C3    THE NEXT TWO LINES READ THE SYMBOLS TO BE USED IN THE GRAPH.  THE PROGRAM
C     MUST BE FOLLOWED BY A DATA CARD CONTAINING, IN ITS FIRST 7 COLUMNS, B.X12*0
C     WHERE B REPRESENTS A BLANK.
      READ 1,BLANK,DOT,X,ONE,TWO,STAR,OH
    1 FORMAT(7A1)
      PRINT 101
  101 FORMAT('1',42X,'READ POSITIVE X DOWN, POSITIVE Y RIGHT'/)
C4    START THE PROGRAM AT THE LEFT END POINT OF THE DOMAIN.
      Z=A
C5    I IS A COUNTER.  TO SMOOTH THE PLOT, Y IS COMPUTED ON ALTERNATE INCREMENTS
C     OF Z.  TO ELIMINATE THIS, REPLACE LINES 57-61 BY GO TO 5.
    5 I=0
C6    PRINT THE Y-AXIS.  THE CRITERION DEPENDS ON THE SIZE OF THE Z INCREMENT.
      IF(ABS(Z).LT..1)GOTO2
C7    THERE ARE 7 PRINTING POSITIONS FOR EACH Y-UNIT.  7 SCALES, .5 ROUNDS.
      L=7.*Y(Z)+.5
C8    COMPUTE THE SYMMETRIC VALUES OF THE GRAPH. OMIT J2 FOR FUNCTIONS.
      J1=61+L
      J2=61-L
C9    (A) ASSIGN A BLANK TO EACH HORIZONTAL SPACE. (B) PLACE A DOT ON THE X-AXIS.
C     (C) WRITE UNIT COORDINATES. (D) ASSIGN POINT DESIGNATOR X TO APPROPRIATE
C     SPACES.  THERE ARE 4 PRINTING LINES PER X-UNIT.  THE CRITERIA FOR PRINTING
C     1 AND 2 ON THE X-AXIS DEPEND ON THE SIZE OF THE Z INCREMENT.
      DO 3 J=1,121
    3 LINE(J)=BLANK
      LINE(61)=DOT
      IF(ABS(Z-1.).LT..1)LINE(61)=ONE
      IF(ABS(Z-2.).LT..1)LINE(61)=TWO
      M=ABS(B)
      N=ABS(A)
      DO 10 K=3,M
   10 IF(ABS(Z-FLOAT(K)).LT..1)LINE(61)=STAR
      DO 11 K=1,N
   11 IF(ABS(Z+FLOAT(K)).LT..1)LINE(61)=STAR
      LINE(J1)=X
      LINE(J2)=X
    7 PRINT 4,LINE
    4 FORMAT(1X,121A1)
C10   STOP AT RIGHT END POINT OF DOMAIN.
      IF(Z.GE.B)STOP
C11   SEE C5.
      I=I+1
      Z=Z+.25
      IF(I.EQ.2)GOTO5
      DO 8 J=1,121
    8 LINE(J)=BLANK
      LINE(61)=DOT
      GOTO7
C12   THE NEXT 12 LINES PRINT THE Y-AXIS INCLUDING ANY INTERCEPT ON IT.
    2 DO 6 J=1,121
    6 LINE(J)=DOT
      L=7.*Y(Z)+.5
      J1=61+L
      J2=61-L
C13   STAR LOCATIONS MUST BE MULTIPLES OF 7 PRINTING SPACES FROM THE X-AXIS.
      DO 9 J=5,121,7
    9 LINE(J)=STAR
      LINE(61)=OH
      LINE(68)=ONE
      LINE(75)=TWO
      LINE(J1)=X
      LINE(J2)=X
      GOTO7
      END
```

Figure 9-10

In Figure 9-9, note the effect of the output descriptor A10 in conjunction with the input descriptor A1. For example, .(dot) is read into the left-most of the six spaces allowed on the IBM 7094. On output, under the descriptor A10, we get $p - q = 10 - 6 = 4$ blanks followed by the constant .(dot) and five blanks. If other output were to follow .(dot), this five spaces separation would persist. It would be better to use one of the following to achieve the same spacing:

       2 FORMAT(1X,'SYMBOL IS',4X,A1)

or

       2 FORMAT(1X,'SYMBOL is   ',A1)

9E.   The Arithmetic IF.

       Given two real numbers a, b exactly one of the following is true: $a > b$, $a = b$ or $a < b$. In our experience with branching we have usually found it necessary to consider only two alternatives such as $a < b$ or $a \geq b$. However, the FORTRAN statement known as the arithmetic IF allows for the full trichotomy. Its form is:

       $IF(e)n_1,n_2,n_3$

where e is a valid FORTRAN expression and n_1, n_2, n_3 are statement numbers. The arithmetic IF transfers control to the statement numbered n_1 if e is negative, to n_2 if e is zero and to n_3 if e is positive. The statement numbers need not be distinct.

       The arithmetic IF may be used in instances where we have used the logical IF. For example, a transfer of control to statement 21 if A is less than B and to 22 otherwise (i.e., if $A \geq B$) can be accomplished by:

       IF(A-B)21,22,22

This is equivalent to:

       IF(A.LT.B)GO TO 21
       GO TO 22

9F.   The Computed GO TO.

       The computed GO TO provides almost limitless branching. The form is:

       GO TO(N1,N2,$\cdots$,NK),I

Each of the K integers N1,N2,...,NK must be a statement number and I must be a positive integer variable between 1 and K inclusive. If, as the computed GO TO is executed, the value of I is J, then control is transferred to statement NJ.

9G.   Conclusion.

The material contained in this book does not exhaust FORTRAN. What we have covered is adequate for calculus and indeed a wide range of scientific applications.

DO, CONTINUE, READ, the arithmetic IF, the computed GO TO, RETURN and CALL are executable statements. DIMENSION is not. The first line of a subprogram is not an executable statement.

EXERCISES

9-1   The Fibonacci (See Section 6) numbers are formed according to the rule $a_n = a_{n-1} + a_{n-2}$, $a_1 = 1$, $a_2 = 1$. Use a DO loop to compute the first 60 Fibonacci numbers. Stop if any number exceeds 30,000.

9-2   Modify the program in Figure 9-4 so as to plot the graph of
(a) $16x^2 + 25y^2 = 400$ (b) $x + 6 = y^2$ for $-6 \le x \le 3$.

9-3   A polynomial function has the form
$f(x) = a_0 + a_1x + a_2x^2 + \ldots + a_nx^n$. Write a single program to read in the coefficients and plot the graph of f for each of the following cases:

$a_0 = .02500$, $a_1 = .62500$, $a_2 = .00833$, $-5 \le x \le 5$

$a_0 = 1.66667$, $a_1 = -1.66667$, $a_2 = -.33333$, $a_3 = .33333$,
$-3 \le x \le 3$

$a_0 = -2.3256$, $a_1 = -1.1628$, $a_2 = .4667$, $a_3 = .2333$,
$-5 \le x \le 5$.

(A machine efficient way of writing polynomials is given on page 11-120.)

9-4   (a) Review your program for EXERCISE 7-1. Rewrite it using subscripted variables.
(b) Modify the program to output the table entries for 7% interest in the 6th year only.

*9-5   Write a program to read five examination grades for each of
        28 students. Compute each student's average and arrange the
        averages in descending order.

*9-6   In EXERCISE 9-5 assume that each student is identified by a
        number (not necessarily the numbers 1 through 28). Have your
        program arrange these student numbers in the same order as
        the grades.

9-7   Using your program (modified) for computing square roots
        (EXERCISE 3-3(a) or EXERCISE 6-3) as a function subprogram
        (don't call it SQRT) rewrite EXERCISE 8-2 to use it rather than
        the supplied SQRT.

9-8   Rewrite the program for EXERCISE 5-5 using DO loops.

9-9   Rewrite the program for EXERCISE 5-6 using DO loops.

9-10   Using subscripted variables, of
        two indices, write and run a
        program to compute (not read)
        and print the 45 entries in
        the array at the right. The
        program should be general
        enough to do an n × m array.

1	4	2	4	2	4	2	4	1
4	16	8	16	8	16	8	16	4
2	8	4	8	4	8	4	8	2
4	16	8	16	8	16	8	16	4
1	4	2	4	2	4	2	4	1

9-11   In EXERCISE 8-5 difficulties arose because of the machine
        representation of decimal fractions. These difficulties can
        be overcome by using alphameric input. Using A field
        specification read in, as a string of symbols, a real occupying
        ten columns. Count the number of spaces between the decimal
        point and the first blank. Use this to determine $L = 2K$ and
        then use the "odd number" method to find the square root of the
        real as in EXERCISE 8-5.

---

*The problem of rearranging a sequence of numbers into ascending or
 descending order is nontrivial. However, it is within the grasp of
 the reader who has done most of the earlier programming problems in
 this book.

10. Numerical Evaluation of Integrals.

In your calculus text, you have seen that the concept of
derivative arises from the simple idea of average rate of change of
one quantity with respect to another. The calculation and application
of derivatives to problems of maxima and minima, curve sketching,
rectilinear motion in gravitational fields, etc., provide powerful
tools for analyzing and solving many physical problems. The concept
of the integral arises from the simple idea of area. The extension
of the concept of area from the rectangle to a variety of regions
having curvilinear borders provides another powerful tool for
scientists. Also, both the concept of the derivative and that of the
integral have uses far beyond those noted here.

Part of the power of the integral comes through the beautiful
and surprising result given by the Fundamental Theorem[1] of the Integral
Calculus. However, by definition, the evaluation of a definite
integral of a function f implies a sequence of numerical computations.
The Fundamental Theorem allows this task to be circumvented if f has
an easily expressed antiderivative. The power of the integral concept
is not limited, however, by the requirement to find an antiderivative
for f. This is fortunate because many elementary problems lead to
integrals of functions which do not have simple antiderivatives.
When confronted by such a situation, one may resort to the definition
of the integral as the limit of a sum and with the use of a computer
approximate the limit to within ε. (As we remarked in Section 6,
the computer does not allow arbitrary choices of ε but does allow
choices which are practical in most applied situations.)

Use of the computer calls for an understanding of the definition
of the integral. In fact, a method of demonstrating that the integral
of a function exists is useful in estimating errors in computations.
This demonstration is accomplished through the use of the upper and
lower Riemann sums which we now define. The concept of upper and
lower Riemann sums is of practical as well as theoretical importance.

---

[1] $\displaystyle\int_a^b f(x)\,dx = F(b) - F(a)$, where $F'(x) = f(x)$, i.e., F is an antiderivative of f.

Let P be the partition $P = \{x_0, x_1, \ldots, x_n \mid x_n = a < x_1 < x_2 < \ldots < x_{n-1} < x_n = b\}$. For each i we choose ξ_i' so that $f(\xi_i') = M_i$ is the maximum[1] value of f on the subinterval $[x_{i-1}, x_i]$. Let $\Delta x_i = x_i - x_{i-1}$. We then form the <u>upper Riemann sum</u>:

$$R_n = \sum_{i=1}^{n} f(\xi_i') \Delta x_i = \sum_{i=1}^{n} M_i \Delta x_i .$$

Similarly, if we choose ξ_i'' so that $f(\xi_i'') = m_i$ is the minimum[1] value of f on each subinterval $[x_{i-1}, x_i]$, we form the <u>lower Riemann sum</u>:

$$r_n = \sum_{i=1}^{n} f(\xi_i'') \Delta x_i = \sum_{i=1}^{n} m_i \Delta x_i .$$

For any other choice ξ_i from $[x_{i-1}, x_i]$ the sum $S_n = \sum_{i=1}^{n} f(\xi_i) \Delta x_i$ is called, simply, a Riemann sum. Clearly, for any choice of ξ_i from the subinterval $[x_{i-1}, x_i]$, we have $m_i \leq f(\xi_i) \leq M_i$. Therefore, $r_n \leq S_n \leq R_n$ where S_n is any Riemann sum corresponding to the partition $P = \{x_0, x_1, \ldots, x_n \mid x_0 = a < x_1 < x_2 < \ldots < x_n = b\}$.

The theoretical importance of the upper and lower Riemann sums derives from the application of the Squeeze Theorem to the last inequality.

If one of the subintervals defined by P, say $[x_{k-1}, x_k]$, is further partitioned into $[x_{k-1}, x_k^*]$, $[x_k^*, x_k]$, where $x_{k-1} < x_k^* < x_k$, we generate what is called a <u>refinement</u> of P. Since the union of $[x_{k-1}, x_k^*]$ and $[x_k^*, x_k]$ is $[x_{k-1}, x_k]$, it is clear that the maximum value of f on either $[x_{k-1}, x_k^*]$ or $[x_k^*, x_k]$ does not exceed $f(\xi_k')$ and on one of them may be less than $f(\xi_k')$. Thus, with increasing n, $\{R_n\}$ is a monotone decreasing sequence. Similarly, $\{r_n\}$ is a monotone increasing sequence. Furthermore, $\{R_n\}$ is bounded below by, say r_1; and $\{r_n\}$ is bounded above by, say R_1. Hence, both the sequences $\{R_n\}$ and $\{r_n\}$ converge. If they can be shown to converge to the same limit, the squeeze theorem will assure us that $\{S_n\}$ converges to this limit also.

If f is continuous on the closed interval $[a,b]$ then for each $\varepsilon > 0$, let $\varepsilon_1 = \dfrac{\varepsilon}{b-a}$, $\varepsilon_1 > 0$. It can be proved that there is a $\delta > 0$ such that

$$|f(x_1) - f(x_2)| < \varepsilon$$

---

[1] We suppose that f is sufficiently nice as to have this property. Specifically, we may require that f be continuous.

for every[1] x_1, x_2 from [a,b] chosen so that

$$|x_1 - x_2| < \delta .$$

Now let us construct P so that the max $(x_i - x_{i-1}) < \delta$. (This can obviously be done by taking, for example, n subintervals of equal length where $n > [1/\delta] + 1$.) With this choice of P we will have $f(\xi_i') - f(\xi_i'') < \varepsilon$ and $f(\xi_i')\Delta x_i - f(\xi_i'')\Delta x_i < \varepsilon_1 \Delta x_i$. From this it follows that

$$R_n - r_n < \varepsilon_1(b - a)$$

since $\sum\limits_{i=1}^{n} \Delta x_i = b - a$. Thus, the difference between the successive terms of $\{R_n\}$ and $\{r_n\}$ can be made as small as we wish by taking the points of P sufficiently close together. But then both $\{R_n\}$ and $\{r_n\}$ and, by the squeeze theorem, $\{S_n\}$ have a common limit. This limit is called the (definite) integral of f on the interval [a,b]. It is denoted by

$$\int_a^b f(x)\,dx .$$

Note that we have not actually set down a method of computing this limit. In some cases, such a method is provided by the Fundamental Theorem of Calculus. However, by computing the successive terms of the sequences of upper and lower Riemann sums until the difference $R_n - r_n$ is smaller than, say ε, we know that both R_n and r_n approximate $\int_a^b f(x)\,dx$ with accuracy ε.

It should be noted that computing the upper and lower Riemann sums R_n and r_n can be quite difficult since they require the determination of values ξ_i' and ξ_i'' which yield the maximum and minimum values of f(x) in each subinterval $[x_{i-1},x_i]$. However, if f is an increasing function on [a,b] ξ_i' and ξ_i'' are respectively the right-hand and left-hand endpoints of $[x_{i-1},x_i]$. If f is decreasing on [a,b], the order is reversed. In some cases where f is not monotone, [a,b] can be partitioned initially into subintervals, say [a,c], [c,d],..., [g,b], on each of which f is monotone.

------

[1]This important property may appear to be obvious. It is a statement of the definition of <u>uniform</u> continuity and follows from the Theorem: "Every function which is continuous on a closed interval is uniformly continuous there." The theorem is usually proved only in more advanced texts.

Here we have been interested in discussing the upper and lower Riemann sums both for their usefulness in substantiating the applicability and convergence of the Riemann sums and for their direct applicability in approximating integrals using a computer. Unfortunately, these sums are rather inefficient for the latter purpose. Figure 1-5 gives a program which computes the integral of an increasing function using the difference $R_n - r_n$ as a criterion. It will be recalled that a partition of more than 4000 subdivisions was required in that program to obtain 3-place accuracy.

The approximation of integrals by upper and lower Riemann sums, by Riemann sums, by the Trapezoidal Rule[1] or by Simpson's Rule[1] gives an introduction to the subject of numerical integration. Numerical integration is also part of the subject referred to elsewhere as Numerical Analysis. Numerical integration is concerned with the derivation of methods for approximating integrals. Our previous computations with various methods of numerical integration have taught us to expect considerable variation in the number of computations necessary to achieve a certain accuracy. Said differently, we can expect that a fixed number of computations will produce different accuracies under different methods of numerical integration. Estimation of these accuracies (or inaccuracies) is obviously an important question.

Usually, direct estimates of the errors incurred in numerical integrations are impossible. However, bounds on the error may be found. Derivation of the formulas for these error bounds is usually reserved for more advanced courses. Here we merely give the formulas for the types of numerical integration discussed in this section and show how to use them to control errors as much as possible.

Our first numerical integration, given in Figure 1-5, is, as we have previously remarked, an example of a lower sum approximation. It can be shown that if [a,b] is subdivided into equal subintervals of length h, then there is an η, $a < \eta < b$, such that the error[2] in such an approximation is given by $\frac{(b-a)h}{2} \cdot f'(\eta)$.

---

[1] See your text.

[2] For a complete discussion see, e.g.: Elementary Numerical Analysis, S. D. Conte, McGraw Hill, 1965.

Such errors are also associated with the other numerical techniques which we have mentioned. For the trapezoidal rule the error[1] is given by $\frac{(b-a)h^2}{12} \cdot f''(\eta)$ for some η, $a < \eta < b$; for Simpson's rule the error is given by $\frac{(b-a)h^4}{180} \cdot f^{(4)}(\eta)$ where again $a < \eta < b$,

The theorems which support these claims are called <u>existence theorems</u>. They tell us that such an η exists. Unfortunately, we do not usually know how to determine η. Thus, we can not usually use these formulas to compute the error in the corresponding type of approximation. However, if we replace the derivatives in these expressions by maxima of their absolute values on the interval $[a,b]$ we obtain bounds on the errors.

Let us compare the errors E_R, E_T, E_S incurred for a partition P of 1000 equally spaced points under rectangular, trapezoidal and Simpson approximations, respectively. Suppose we seek $\int_1^3 (x^3 - 1)dx$ numerically. Now $f'(x) = 3x^2$ so that a bound on the error using a rectangular approximation is $\frac{\max|3x^2|}{500}$. $f''(x) = 6x$ and an error bound using a trapezoidal approximation is $\frac{2 \cdot \max|6x|}{3 \times 10^6}$. Since $\max|3x^2| = 27$ on $[1,3]$ and $\max|6x| = 18$ there, we have $E_R = .054$ while $E_T = .000048$. That is, the error bound for a rectangular approximation is about one thousand times as large as the error bound for the trapezoidal approximation for the integrand used in this example.

Surprisingly, $E_S = 0$. In fact, a little reflection on the form of the error term will convince the reader that Simpson's rule gives an exact evaluation of any integral whose integrand is a linear, quadratic or cubic function.

An alternate use of the error term is to help us decide how many points we should use in a partition P. That is, the error term can help us decide how small h must be. Recall that $h = (b-a)/n$. Using this, our error terms become, respectively, $\frac{(b-a)^2 f'(\eta)}{2n}$, $\frac{(b-a)^3 f''(\eta)}{12n^2}$ and $\frac{(b-a)^5 f^{(4)}(\eta)}{90n^4}$. If we choose n so that:

---

[1] Again see <u>Elementary Numerical Analysis</u>, S. D. Conte, McGraw Hill, 1965.

$$\frac{(b-a)^2 \max|f'(x)|}{2n} < \varepsilon$$

or

$$\frac{(b-a)^3 \max|f''(x)|}{12n^2} < \varepsilon$$

or

$$\frac{(b-a)^5 \max|f^{(4)}(\eta)|}{180n^4} < \varepsilon$$

the error due to our approximation technique will be smaller than ε. Thus, for a rectangular approximation to produce an error less than 10^{-4} in approximating $\int_1^3 (x^3 - 1)\,dx$, P should contain about 540,000 points while for a trapezoidal approximation a partition containing only about 335 points will suffice. (The reader should carry out the necessary computations to verify these facts using the last two inequalities.) Hence, trapezoidal approximation appears more economical in computing time than rectangular approximation and the results will be much less influenced by roundoff error. The partition required by Simpson's rule need contain only 3 points, 1, 2 and 3!

Thus, to achieve the accuracy required in Figure 1-5, we must find $|f'(x)|$ on $[2,5]$. We find $|f'(x)| < 1$. Therefore, to achieve an accuracy of .001 it is sufficient to have $(b-a)^2/2n < .001$. Solving for n, we find $n > 4500$. Note the agreement of this result with that found in Figure 1-6. (If an accuracy of 10^{-6} were required, 4.5×10^6 subdivisions would be required. Roundoff, as discussed in Section 8, would probably preclude this degree of accuracy.) Application of the trapezoidal rule would require only about 11 subdivisions and Simpson's rule about 4^1 subdivisions. The reader should verify these results and reprogram Figure 1-5 for trapezoidal and Simpson approximations. Why will it not be necessary to have a line like 35?

The reader is referred to the EXERCISES at the end of this section for further problems involving the use of these error terms. Rectangular approximations are not useful computing devices (unless

---

[1]Actually, n must be an even integer greater than 3.7.

max$|f'(x)|$ is small) in spite of the fact that the upper and lower
Riemann sums, which are special rectangular approximations, can be
used to prove that the Riemann integral of a function continuous on
a closed interval exists.

Other methods[1] of numerical integration are studied in courses
in Numerical Analysis.

Finally, we remark that the problems of accumulated roundoff may
be lessened by the use of DOUBLE PRECISION variables and constants
which we discussed in Section 8.

EXERCISES

10-1   (a)   Write and run a program for a trapezoidal approximation

to $\int_{2}^{5} \ln(x^2 + 5)\,dx$ using 11 equal subintervals.

(b)   Do the same using Simpson's rule with 4 equal subintervals.

(Hint: Recall a technique used in EXERCISE 3-1(d).)

10-2   Verify the values of   n   referred to in EXERCISE 10-1.

10-3   In each of the following a function   f   is given on an interval
        [a,b].   For each find the number, n, of subdivisions required
        to achieve an accuracy of 10^{-4} in rectangular, trapezoidal
        and Simpson approximations to the integral of the given function:
        (a) $f(x) = x + 1/x$, $[\frac{1}{2},4]$;   (b) $f(x) = x/(x^2 + 1)$, $[0,2]$;
        (c) $f(x) = x + 2\sqrt{2 + x}$, $[-1,7]$.

10-4   Using upper and lower sums approximate $\int_{1}^{2} dx/x$.   Use equal
        intervals, halving their lengths on each successive
        approximation.   At each step write out the number of sub-
        divisions and the values of both upper and lower sums.   Continue
        until $R_n - r_n < 5.E - 6$ or the number of subdivisions is
        greater than 1.E5.   Do the same problem in DOUBLE PRECISION and
        print the results side by side.   Write appropriate table headings.

---

[1]See e.g. Elementary Numerical Analysis by S. D. Conte, McGraw Hill
Book Company.

10-5   Using upper and lower sums approximate π in both single and
double precision by finding the area in the first quadrant
bounded by the circle of radius 2 with center at the origin.
Start with 256 subdivisions and doubling the number of subdivisions on successive passes continue until the difference
between the upper and lower sums is less than 10^{-4} or the
number of subdivisions is greater than 9000. List the results
side by side with appropriate headings.

10-6   Calculate the value of π to 3 decimal places by an appropriate
numerical integration of $1/(1 + x^2)$. Why does your integral
give the value of π?

10-7   An elliptical pool is 17 feet wide and 33 feet long. What is
its circumference to the nearest inch?

10-8   The natural logarithm is defined to be $\ln x = \int_1^x \frac{dt}{t}$. The base
of this system of logarithms is the number e such that $\ln e = 1$.
Use the functions $y = t^n$ for the values of n: $n = 1.01$, .99,
1.001, .999, ... , approaching 1, to approximate e using the

"squeeze theorem". That is, solve $\int_1^x \frac{dt}{t^n} = \frac{x^{1-n} - 1}{1 - n} = 1$ for x

for the indicated values of n approaching 1. Stop when e is
known to five decimal places.

10-9 (Monte Carlo Integration): An interesting approach to evaluating
an integral is the following. Suppose f is continuous and
positive on [a,b] (generalizations will be obvious). Construct
a rectangle of area A with base [a,b] which contains entirely
the area under f. Use a random number generator to pick 10^N
points in the rectangle. Suppose P of them are not outside the
desired area. The value of the integral is approximately
$(P/10^N)A$.

Use this method to evaluate some integrals which you have
previously determined by other methods. (The generation of
random numbers is an extremely difficult problem. See Hamming,
ibid. Often "pseudo random" are used instead. For a
description of the generation of such numbers see Rice and Rice,
ibid. Your Computer Center can probably supply a library
subprogram which generates random numbers.)

10-10   Using the definition of the natural
         logarithm: $\ln x = \int_1^x dx/x$, write
         and run a program to use
         Simpson's rule to complete
         the table at the right.
         Computations should be
         correct to three decimal
         places.

Natural logs						
N	0	1	2	3	...	9
1.0						
1.1						
:						
1.9						

10-11   Write a table of Common logarithms using the same tabular
         format as in EXERCISE 10-10.

10-12   A special form of the comparison theorem for integrals states:
         If f and g are integrable and $f(x) \le g(x)$ on $[0,x]$,
         then $\int_0^x f(t)dt \le \int_0^x g(t)dt$. Apply this repeatedly to the
         inequality: $0 \le \sin x \le x$. This will lead to inequalities
         of the form $f_1(x) \le \cos x \le g_1(x)$ and $f_2(x) \le \sin x \le g_2(x)$
         where f_1 and g_1 are polynomials of even powers and f_2
         and g_2 are polynomials of odd powers. Obtain polynomial
         approximations to the sine and cosine of degree 7 and 8
         respectively.

10-13   Using the above polynomials write and run a program to print
         a table of values of sine and cosine, correct to five decimal
         places, for angles of 1°, 2°, 3°,...,45°. Write your program
         to include appropriate headings.

11.   Applications to Functions Two Variables, Infinite Series

That a functional value can be determined by two, or more, variables is no surprise. Our purpose in this section is not simply to evaluate such functions - that we have done before. Rather, we want to discuss some introductory numerical techniques for solving some of the problems which arise in the calculus of several variables. We restrict our attention to functions of the form $z = z(x,y)$, i.e., explicit functions of two variables.

11A.   The maximum or minimum of a function of two variables.

As the reader is aware, the requirement to find a local maximum or a local minimum of a function of two variables presents more computational difficulty than does the corresponding problem for functions of one variable. The necessary condition is that the derivatives $f_x(x,y) = f_y(x,y) = 0$. In general finding an x_0, y_0 for which these are true is computationally difficult.

We avoid these difficulties by substituting a "hill-climbing" method based on the gradient. As you know from your calculus text, the direction of the gradient is the direction of greatest functional change. The value of the function is increasing in the direction of the gradient when the directional derivative is positive in that direction and decreasing when it is negative. While we could "climb" along any succession of paths with positive directional derivatives, using the direction of the gradient is clearly most efficient.

The procedure is as follows. Choose a point (x_0, y_0) sufficient-ly near the (x,y) coordinates of the maximum or minimum. Compute new coordinates (x_1, y_1) h units from (x_0, y_0) in the direction of the gradient or opposite to that direction as appropriate. Repeat this operation until the desired extremum is reached. Of course, the signal that the extremum has been reached is the reversal of the direction of the gradient.

The accuracy with which the (x,y) coordinates of the extremum are approximated depends upon the size of h. Therefore, h should be dictated by the desired accuracy. On the other hand, a small h may require excessive computer time. A compromise is to start with a relatively large h and decrease it near the extremum. For example,

each time the direction of the gradient reverses the value of h could
be reduced. The reductions could continue until the extremum is
located to within the required accuracy.

11B. Numerical evaluation of double integrals over rectangles.

To introduce this subject, let us interpret the double integral
as a volume. We can interpret the integral in the following way.

Let $z(x,y)$ be defined and positive on R, a rectangle in the
xy-plane. Consider a cross section parallel to, say, the xz-plane
of the three dimensional region (volume) under $z(x,y)$. Denote this
cross-sectional area by $A(y)$. The double integral over the
rectangle is $\int A(y)\,dy$ between the appropriate limits. In your calculus
text this leads to the concept of the iterated integral.

By now it is easily conceivable to the reader that it may be
impossible to derive a simple formula for $A(y)$ or, having one, to
find an antiderivative for $A(y)$. If we have a formula for $A(y)$,
then the evaluation of $\iint z(x,y)\,dx\,dy$ becomes simply the evaluation,
possibly numerically, of $\int A(y)\,dy$. We discussed several elementary
techniques using rectangles, trapezoids and parabolas in Section 10.
Therefore, we have reduced the problem to one previously solved and
say nothing more about it here (but see EXERCISES).

Even if we can not find a formula for $A(y)$ we can numerically
approximate $\iint z(x,y)\,dx\,dy$. The underlying procedure is apparent after
a little thought. What is needed to evaluate $\int A(y)\,dy$ numerically
is a set of values of $A(y)$ at reasonably spaced intervals along the
y-axis. Then a numerical integration of $A(y)$ can be undertaken.
However, it matters not if this set of values is obtained by evaluating
a formula for $A(y)$ or by a prior numerical integration over x for
each of the selected values of y. We now can develop certain formulas.

Let $z = z(x,y)$ be defined and positive on R as in Figure 11-1.
For fixed y_2, the area $A(y_2)$ of the intersection of the region
under the surface $z = z(x,y)$ with the plane $y = y_2$ can be
determined by various techniques. If $\int_{x_0}^{x_1} z(x,y_2)\,dx$ can be evaluated
be the fundamental theorem of calculus, then this value is $A(y_2)$.
If these integrals can be evaluated for all $y, \ y_0 \le y \le y$, then the
volume is given by $\int_{y_0}^{y_1} A(y)\,dy$. This, of course, is the method of
iterated integrals.

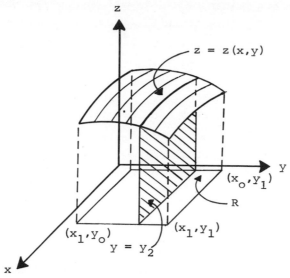

Figure 11-1

If $\int_{x_0}^{x_1} z(x,y_2)\,dx$ is not amenable to attack by the fundamental theorem, then it may be approximated numerically in a manner analogous to the one variable case previously studied.

An analogue to the trapezoidal rule would be described as follows. We choose an n and devide the interval $[y_0,y_1]$ into n subintervals of length $h = (y_1 - y_0)/n$. We then consider the n + 1 functions $z(x,y_0)$, $z(x,\ y_0 + h)$, $z(x,\ y_0 + 2h),\ldots,\ z(x,y_1)$. The areas of the n + 1 plane regions under the graphs of $z = z(x,\ y_0 + ih)$ in the planes $y = y_0 + ih\ (i = 0,1,2,\ldots,n)$ for x such that $x_0 \le x \le x_1$ give n + 1 cross sections of the required volume. Since we suppose that these areas cannot be determined by the fundamental theorem, each of them must be approximated by some numerical technique. We choose here to describe how to do this by the trapezoidal rule. We choose an m (m may be different from the n chosen above) and apply the trapezoidal rule in the usual way to each of the n + 1 functions $z(x,\ y_0 + ih)$ discussed above. The result is n + 1 values of $A(y)$ determined at the equally spaced values of y: y_0, $y_0 + h$, $y_0 + 2h,\ldots,y_1$. These values can then be then be used to obtain a trapezoidal approximation to $\int_{y_0}^{y_1} A(y)\,dy$.

It is possible to work out a formula for this two-dimensional analogue to trapezoidal approximation. This is left as an exercise for the reader. However, it is recommended that this derivation be delayed until after reading the derivation of a two dimensional analogue to Simpson's Rule which we discuss next.

Again let $z(x,y)$ be defined on R as in Figure 11-1. For fixed y_2, the area $A(y_2)$ of the intersection of the region under z with the plane $y = y_2$ is given by a three point Simpson's Rule as:

$$A(y_2) = \frac{h}{3} [z(x_0,y_2) + 4z(x_0 + h, y_2) + z(x_0 + 2h, y_2)]$$

where $h = (x_1 - x_0)/2$.

If we now evaluate $A(y_0)$, $A(y_0 + k)$, $A(y_0 + 2k)$ where $k = (y_1 - y_0)/2$ by this method, we can approximate the volume of the region under z by a three point Simpson's Rule as

$$V = \frac{k}{3} [A(y_0) + 4A(y_0 + k) + A(y_0 + 2k)] \quad \text{where } k = (y_1 - y_0)/2.$$

Combining the numerical integration over x with that over y we obtain

$$V = \frac{hk}{9} [z(x_0,y_0) + 4z(x_0 + h, y_0) + z(x_0 + 2h, y_0) +$$

$$4(z(x_0,y_0+ k) + 4z(x_0 + h, y_0 + k) + z(x_0 + 2h, y_0 + k)) +$$

$$z(x_0,y_0 + 2k) + 4z(x_0 + h, y_0 + k) + z(x_0 + 2h, y_0 + 2k)]$$

$$= \frac{hk}{9} [z(x_0,y_0) + 4z(x_0 + h, y_0) + z(x_0 + 2h, y_0) +$$

$$4z(x_0,y_0 + k) + 16z(x_0 + h, y_0 + k) + 4z(x_0 + 2h, y_0 + k) +$$

$$z(x_0,y_0 + 2k) + 4z(x_0 + h, y_0 + 2k) + z(x_0 + 2h, y_0 + 2k)] \ .$$

This is called a "nine point" Simpson's Rule. It is a two dimensional analogue to the Simpson's Rule discussed in Section 10.

Naturally, in order to achieve a satisfactory degree of accuracy, we must be able to use arbitrarily many points (and, hence, arbitrarily small h) rather than just three in each direction as we have above. We can see how to do this by studying the correspondence between the points used above and the corresponding coefficent array as shown in Figure 11-2.

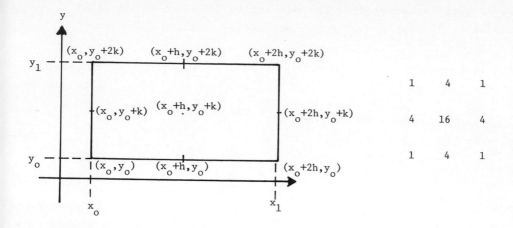

Figure 11-2

We can cascade these nine point formulas in both the x and y directions. For example, the 15 points in Figure 11-3 are treated as two arrays of nine points in Figure 11-4.

$y_0 + 2k$.   .   .   .   .

$y_0 + k$.   .   .   .   .

y_0 .   .   .   .   .

x_0 x_0+h x_0+2h x_0+3h x_0+4k

Figure 11-3

$y_0 + 2k$.   .   . $y_0 + 2k$.   .   .

$y_0 + k$.   .   . $y_0 + k$.   .   .

y_0 .   .   . y_0 .   .   .

x_0 x_0+h x_0+2h x_0+2h x_0+3h x_0+4h

Figure 11-4

Note the repetition of the column labelled x_o + 2h. To approximate V over the above 15 point array we apply the nine-point formula to each of the nine point arrays in Figure 11-4 and obtain

$$V = \frac{hk}{9}[\text{previous expression}] + \frac{hk}{9}[z(x_o+2h,y_o) + 4z(x_o+3h,y_o) + z(x_o+4h,y_o) +$$

$$4z(x_o+2h,y_o+k) + 16(x_o+3h,y_o+k) + 4z(x_o+4h,y_o+k) +$$

$$z(x_o+2h,y_o+2k) + 4z(x_o+3h,y_o+2k) + z(x_o+4h,y_o+2k)]$$

Combining these we get

$$V = \frac{hk}{9}[z(x_o,y_o) + 4z(x_o+h,y_o) + 2z(x_o+2h,y_o) + 4z(x_o+3h,y_o) + z(x_o+4h,y_o) +$$

$$4z(x_o,y_o+k) + 16z(x_o+h,y_o+k) + 8z(x_o+2h,y_o+k) + 16z(x_o+3h,y_o+k) + 4z(x_o+4h,y_o+k) +$$

$$z(x_o,y_o+2k) + 4z(x_o+h,y_o+2k) + 2z(x_o+2h,y_o+2k) + 4z(x_o+3h,y_o+2k) + z(x_o+4h,y_o+2k)]$$

The coefficient array for this expression is given in Figure 11-5.

1	4	2	2	1
4	16	8	16	4
1	4	2	4	1

Figure 11-5

This array can be thought of as being constructed by overlapping two arrays such as on the right in Figure 11-2 and adding the elements which overlap. This cascading can be continued both horizontally and vertically. A 7x7 array built in this way is

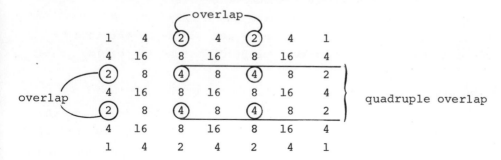

Figure 11-6

The $(2m + 1)$ x $(2n + 1)$ array of points in Figure 11-7

$y_0 + 2mk$ ⋮ · · · · · · ·

$y_0 + 3k$ · · · · · ·

$y_0 + 2k$ · · · · · ·

$y_0 + k$ · · · · · ... ·

y_0 · · · · · ... ·

x_0 $x_0 + h$ $x_0 + 2h$ $x_0 + 3h$ $x_0 + 4h$ $x_0 + 2nh$

Figure 11-7

leads to the coefficient array in Figure 11-8.

1	4	2	4	2	...	4	1
⋮							
4	16	8	16	8	...	16	4
2	8	4	8	4	...	8	2
4	16	8	16	8	...	16	4
1	4	2	4	2	...	4	1

Figure 11-8

The error bound given in Section 10 for Simpson's Rule can be applied here in each direction. However, the computations can become quite involved so we do not insist on them. To find a suitable h, for example, we would need the maximum value over x and y of $\partial^4 z/\partial x^4$ and for k the maximum value of $\partial^4 z/\partial y^4$. As we have remarked earlier in this section, these maxima may be obtained by a numerical method. Similar procedures hold for the trapezoidal rule.

11C. Surface Area.

Your calculus text gives an integral formula for computing the area of a surface $z = z(x,y)$ over a region R in the xy plane. Generally speaking, these integrals cannot be evaluated by applying the fundamental theorem to the iterated integrals involved because of the impossibility of finding antiderivatives for the integrands. As we have seen earlier in this section, we can approximate these integrals by a two-dimensional trapezoidal rule or Simpson's Rule.

In this short subsection, however, we comment briefly on another method of approximating surface area. Again we suppose the area in question is defined over a rectangle region R in the xy plane.

We use the fact that three points determine a plane. If these three points are in the surface, then the plane triangle which they determine is "close" to the surface and its vertices are in the surface. To generate such triangles in a systematic way, subdivide R as shown in Figure 11-9 and compute the coordinates, on the surface

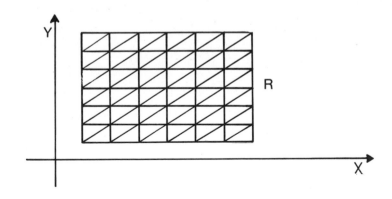

Figure 11-9

of the projections of the vertices of the triangles in this subdivision of R.   The points given by these coordinates are the vertices
of approximating triangles. The sum of the areas of the collection
of all such triangles forms an approximation to the area of the surface
over R.   Note that the triangles involved neither overlap or leave
holes. The approximating surface created by any one subdivision of
R resembles the famous geodesic dome created by Buckminster Fuller.
Obviously, the accuracy of the approximation depends upon the smallness
of the triangular approximants.

Unfortunately, this intuitively reasonable method does not
necessarily converge to the surface area as the number of triangles
increases even if they all are shrinking in a uniform way. In fact
it can be shown that the method gives the wrong value for such a
simple surface as a right circular cylinder of radius r and height h^1.
It is presented here both as an interesting computational problem and
as further illustration of the value of the Squeeze Theorem in assuring
convergence.

11D. Infinite Series.

Infinite series are studied in your calculus text. We do not
repeat the theory here. We do, however, recall our remarks in
Section 6 concerning the impossibility of achieving arbitrary smallness
or performing certain operations more than a finite number of times on
the computer. Therefore, in applying the computer in the evaluation
of infinite series we must again be content with an approximation
which is obtained by summing the terms toward the beginning of the
series (say the first 50, 100 or 10000 terms).

As we know from Taylor's theorem, we can express any function
which has a suitable number of derivatives, as a polynomial plus a
remainder. As is clear from Lagrange's form of the remainder, the
magnitude of the error in a polynomial approximation increases as the
(n + 1)st power of the length of the interval over which we are
summing the series (polynomial approximation). Thus, it is important
to keep this interval short. If, on the other hand, computation over
a large interval is required, as for example in the computation of a
table of sine values, it may be necessary to program several different
expansions distributed over the interval.

---

[1]See: Surface Area by L. Cesari, Princeton University Press, 1956
  (page 25).

Computing the value of a polynomial of high degree, such as the first k terms of a power series representation of some function, also requires considerable planning in order to economize on machine time. One approach, called Horner's method, is to write

$$f(x) = a_0 + a_1x + a_2x^2 + \ldots + a_nx^n$$

in the form

$$f(x) = (\cdots(((a_nx + a_{n-1})x + a_{n-2})x + \cdots)x + a_0 \; .$$

This form is equivalent to

$$b_1 = a_nx + a_{n-1}$$

$$b_2 = b_1x + a_{n-2}$$

$$b_3 = b_2x + a_{n-3}$$

.
.
.

$$f(x) = b_{n-1}x + a_0 \qquad .$$

The advantage of this is that the former expression requires $\sum_{k=1}^{n} k$ multiplications whereas the latter requires only n multiplications. The efficiency is seen rather dramatically by evaluating a high degree polynomial with and without the use of Horner's method using a hand held calculator.

EXERCISES

11-1   Use the method of gradients to find, correct to three decimal places, the (x,y) coordinates of the local minimum of the following functions near the indicated values (start with h = .1):

(a) $f(x,y) = x^2 + xy + y^2$, near $(-1,2)$.

(b) $f(x,y) = \sin^2(2x^4 - 4x^3y + 3x^2(2y^2 + 1) - 3xy + 3y^2 - 4xy^3 + 2y^4)$
near $(1,1)$.

(c) $f(x,y) = x^4 - 2x^2y^2 + y^4 + x^2 + y^2 - 2x + 4$, inside
$(x - \tfrac{1}{2})^2 + (y - \tfrac{1}{2})^2 = 1.$

11-2. Using 12 subdivision in both x and y directions, use the two dimensional Simpson's Rule to approximate

$$\int_0^2 \int_0^2 (16 - x^2 - y^2)^{-1/2} \, dxdy.$$

11-3 Work out a coefficient array for a 2-dimensional "trapezoidal" rule with m subdivisions in the y-direction and n subdivisions in the x-direction.

11-4 Evaluate:

(a) $\int_{-1}^2 \int_2^3 (x^2 + y^2 + 1)^{1/3} xdxdy,$ (b) $\int_0^2 \int_1^4 e^{x^2+y^2} dxdy .$

11-5 Using the triangularization method described in Section 11C, approximate the area of the surface $z = \sqrt{9 - x^2 - y^2}$ over the square $0 \le x \le 2$, $0 \le y \le 2$. Let the vertices of the triangles be defined by subdividing the 2-unit square into $2n^2$ triangles, each being half of n^2 subsquares. Start with $n = 2$ and continue subdividing until two successive approximations differ by less than 10^{-4} or until all triangles in one approximation to the surface have area less than 10^{-3}. (Recall EXERCISE 7-5).

11-6 Program the example cited in Surface Area (see footnote page 11-119) and by varying the parameters, obtain various results.

11-7 If a table of cosx, $0 \le x \le \pi$, is to be computed using no more than 5 terms of the Taylor expansion of cosx, how many expansions will suffice?

11-8 Write a program to compute a table of sines of angles from 0° to 45° at intervals of 10'.

11-9   Use a series expansion of $\ln(1 + x)$ to write a program to compute a table of natural logarithms of numbers from 1 to 1.99 at intervals of .01. Arrange the output in tabular form like that in EXERCISE 10-10. Compare this program with the one for EXERCISE 10-10. Compare the times required. Computations should be correct to three decimal places.

11-10   A theorem which is often omitted from beginning calculus texts but which illustrates the importance of absolute convergence is the following.

Theorem (Riemann): The terms of a conditionally convergent series of real terms may be rearranged so as to produce a sequence of partial sums converging to any specified real number.

(a) Apply this theorem to the alternating harmonic series $\sum_{n=1}^{\infty} (-1)^{n+1}/n$ so as to produce a sequence of partial sums converging to 2. (Hint: sum, sequentially, the positive terms until 2 is exceeded. Then, subtract the largest negative term not already used. Continue.)

(b) Print the number of positive terms added each time in order to obtain a partial sum exceeding 2.

(c) Guided by part (a), sketch a proof of Riemann's Theorem.

11-11   In the study of infinite series you have occasionally shown that either a series diverges or that convergence tests fail. In some of these cases it was not easy to see that the series "actually" diverged. That is, the intuition was left unsatisfied

(a) Show that $\sum_{n=10}^{\infty} \frac{1}{n \, \mathrm{log} n}$ diverges. Compare this result with the so-called p-series. What do you conclude about the growth of log x as compared with x^{α} for $\alpha > 0$? The graph of $y = x^{.01}$ crosses the graph of $y = \log x$ at about x = 2.8. Do the graphs again cross? What if they don't? The largest numbers which a computer can handle are of the order of 10^{38} on the IBM 7094 and of the order of 10^{308} on the CDC 6500. Can the computer be used to find an x for which $x^{.01} > \log x$? If so, how?

(b)   Show that $\sum\limits_{n=1}^{\infty} \dfrac{(1.01)^n}{n^{1.01}}$ diverges.   In fact, show that

any series of the form $\sum\limits_{n=1}^{\infty} \dfrac{a^n}{n^a}$, $a > 1$, diverges.

11-12   Suppose $(x,y,f(x,y))$ defines a surface S for x, y is
rectangle R in the x, y plane.   It can be shown that if
f_x and f_y are continuous on R, then the area of S is
given by

$$S = \iint\limits_{R} \sqrt{1 + f_x^2 + f_y^2} \; dx \; dy$$

(a)   Apply this formula to find the area of the surface
$z = \sqrt{2xy}$ over the rectangle $1 \le x \le 3, \; 1 \le y \le 2$.

(b)   Using eight subdivisions in each direction, apply the
two-dimensional Simpson's rule of this section to
approximate the area of this surface.

11-13   Apply the formula given in EXERCISE 11-12 to find, correct to
four places, the area of the surface $z = \frac{1}{3}x^3 + y$.   (Hint:
Set up the iterated integrals for the area.   Carry out one
integration using the Fundamental Theorem.   Then use Simpson's
rule for one variable with 16 subdivisions to approximate the
other.)

11-14   Using the formula for the error in Simpson's rule, verify the
appropriateness of using 16 subdivisions in EXERCISE 11-13.

11-15   Apply EXERCISE 11-13 to the surface $z = \frac{1}{4}y^4 + \frac{2}{3}x^{3/2}$.   Use
24 subdivisions.

11-16   The gradient method of EXERCISE 11-1 can also be used to solve
systems of nonlinear equations.   A solution to the system of
equations $f(x,y) = c$, $g(x,y) = d$ gives the minimum of
$(f(x,y) - c)^2 + (g(x,y) - d)^2$.   Use this idea to solve the
system:

$$\begin{cases} x^3 - 2.1xy + 3.6y^2 = 27.5 \\ x^3 + y^3 = 31.53 \end{cases}$$

12. Differential Equations.

In this section we consider differential equations of the form:

(1) $$y' = f(x,y), \quad y(x_0) = y_0 .$$

Your calculus or differential equations text will provide you with several examples of such equations which are solvable by modest extensions of the techniques of calculus. Here, we discuss some simple numerical methods by which the solutions of less "nice" differential equations can be approximated.

There are several ways in which even first order differential equations can be difficult to solve. Most non-linear equations do not admit of solutions by the techniques of separation of variables and the application of integrating factors. Even linear, first order differential equations may prove to be intractable if they are non-homogeneous and the forcing terms do not readily reveal their anti-derivatives. However, such differential equations may have solutions ensured by existence theorems. Such theorems assert that, if it satisfies certain conditions, a given differential equation does have a solution which passes through a point of interest, say (x_0,y_0), of the xy-plane. Furthermore, under additional conditions, there is only one such solution - a desirable situation from the point of view of applications.

Unfortunately, the existence theorem (as we have seen before) does not tell us how to find the solution - only that there is one. However, as we have observed before, this knowledge gives us the confidence to try to approximate the solution. In fact some of the existence theorems which you encounter in your calculus or differential equations book may be constructive, that is, they tell how to approximate the solution. We shall not further consider such theorems in this book. After you have explored some of these approximation techniques, you may find the further considerations of existence theorems interesting.

First, we consider a graphical technique which gives us qualitative knowledge of the behavior of the solutions of a differential equation. To start the method, we recall the interpretation of y' as the slope of the tangent to a curve. Now, if y' = f(x,y) has a

solution   y = h(x)   then the slope of its tangent at any point is the
value of   f(x,y) at that point.   Thus, if we know that there is a
solution passing through a point with coordinates (x_0,y_0), we know
that the slope of the tangent to that solution at (x_0,y_0) is given by
$f(x_0,y_0)$.

Suppose that we know that   y' = f(x,y)   has a unique solution
through every point of some region R of the plane.   The region R is
not always the entire plane as we shall see by examples.   To develop
this qualitative view of the solutions to the differential equation (1)
and strengthen our intuitive view of what it means for a differential
equation to have a unique solution through every point of R, we
proceed as follows.   Choose a point of R, say (x_0,y_0), and evaluate
f at that point.   Now, not only plot the point (x_0,y_0) but through it
draw a short segment having $f(x_0,y_0)$ as slope.   This segment is
tangent to the solution to (1) passing through (x_0,y_0).   It is usually
called a <u>line element</u>.   In Figure 12-1, we indicate several line
elements for the differential equation y' = x^2 + y^2.   The collection
of all line elements defined by a differential equation is called a
<u>direction</u> <u>field</u>.

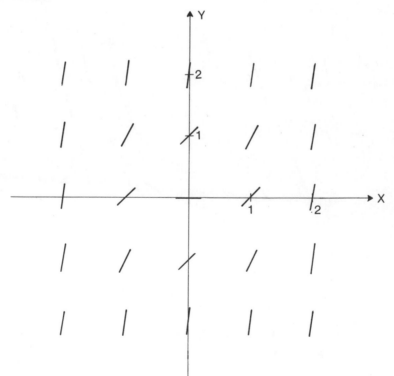

Figure 12-1

From Figure 12-1, we see that the farther we are from the origin the steeper is the inclination of the associated line element. However, it is still difficult to form a firm view of the behavior of the solutions of $y' = x^2 + y^2$.

The additional information about the line elements which organizes the process is found in the method of _isoclines_ (from: iso = same; cline = inclination). That is, we consider the line elements arranged into sets such that all elements of one set of line elements have the same inclination or slope. Each of these sets is, then, characterized by the property $y' = k$. To find the points in R which $y' = k$, we must solve the algebraic equation $f(x,y) = k$. For the example used in Figure 12-1, this becomes $x^2 + y^2 = k$. Thus, at every point of each circle of the family $x^2 + y^2 = k$, the associated line element has the slope k. Each such circle is an isocline. In Figure 12-2, we indicate several isoclines with representative line elements for the present example. Also sketched are approximate solutions suggested by the pattern of the line elements.

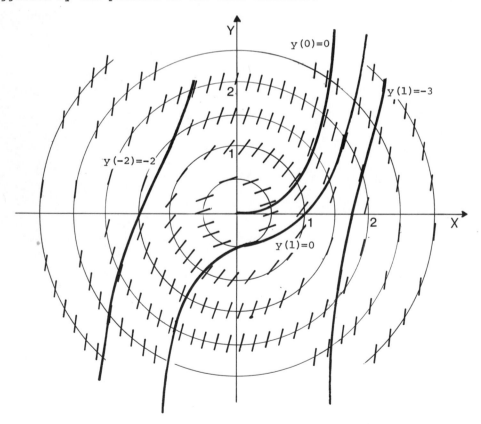

Figure 12-2

We can see by the method of isoclines that R is not the entire plane for some differential equations. For this purpose consider the differential equation $y' = \sqrt{2x + y - 1}$. First of all, we see that the differential equation defines a direction field only if $2x + y - 1 \geq 0$. That is, line elements exist only for those points which are on or above (on or to the right of) the line $y = 1 - 2x$. This line, several isoclines with their associated line elements, and selected approximate solutions are shown in Figure 12-3.

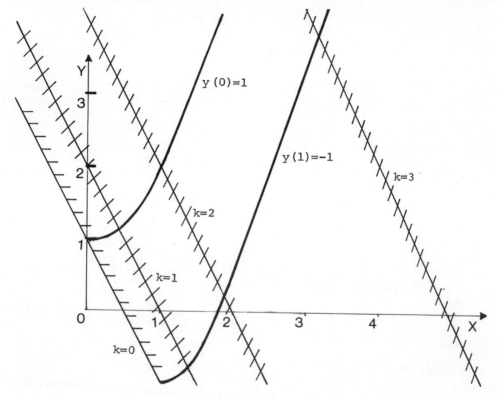

Figure 12-3

Revealing as is the method of isoclines about the qualitative behavior of the solutions of differential equations, it does not satisfy our desire for quantitative information. In particular, we have only intuitive knowledge of how to proceed from one line element to another. Accordingly, we now discuss our first numerical method.

Recall from the study of calculus that the differential of a function gives a linear approximation to the function. This particular linear approximation is the tangent line to the graph of the function. The reader has doubtless used the differential to approximate functions and knows that the magnitude of the error made depends upon the concavity of the function and the distance from the point of tangency. Both claims depend upon the derivative (Lagrange's) form of the remainder term in Taylor's formula.

Using the idea of the differential, we construct a sequence of points (X_n, Y_n) where

$$(2) \qquad \left. \begin{aligned} X_0 &= x_0 \\ Y_0 &= y_0 \\ Y_n &= Y_{n-1} + hf(X_{n-1}, Y_{n-1}) \\ X_n &= x_0 + nh \end{aligned} \right\} \quad n = 1, 2, 3, \ldots$$

It is not hard to see that the recursion formula[1], (2), leads to the construction of a polygonal path. One segment of this path is shown in Figure 12-4. This polygon is an approximation to the solution to

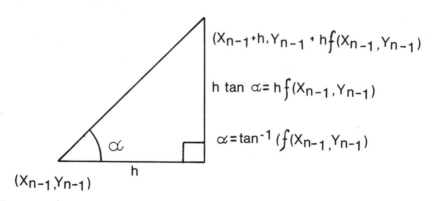

$$(X_{n-1} + h, Y_{n-1} + hf(X_{n-1}, Y_{n-1}))$$

$$h \tan \alpha = hf(X_{n-1}, Y_{n-1})$$

$$\alpha = \tan^{-1}(f(X_{n-1}, Y_{n-1}))$$

(X_{n-1}, Y_{n-1}) h

Figure 12-4

(1) passing through (x_0, y_0). This construction is known as Euler's method. As the reader will see, large values h will cause the polygonal path to diverge widely from the actual solution in most cases. On the other hand, very small values of h will lead to very many calculations with the attendant round off error.

To illustrate the method, we approximate $y(5)$ on the solution to:

$$(3) \qquad y\, dx + x\, dy = 0, \quad y(1) = 1 .$$

The reader will recognize that the variables can be separated in this equation to produce the solution $y = 1/x$. For the sake of comparison, we apply Euler's method to approximate this solution. For an h of

---

[1] In programming (2), the new Y must be computed before X is incremented.

0.5 the comparison is shown in Figure 12-5.   To construct the figure
we rewrite the differential equation (3) in the form of (1), namely,

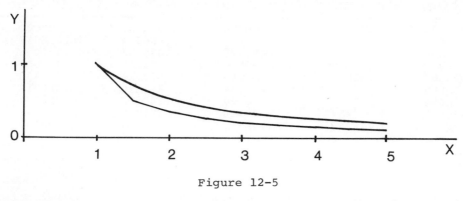

Figure 12-5

(4)   y' = y/x , y(1) = 1 .

The other data which we need to start the recursion (2) are
Y_0 = 1, X_0 = 1, f(X,Y) = -Y/X.   For   y(5), h = 0.5; n = 1,2,...,8.
Using (2), we compute the following Table 12-1.   Table 12-1 is used

TABLE 12-1

n	X_n	Y_n	y_n	Error
1	1.500	0.500	0.667	-.167
2	2.000	0.333	0.500	-.167
3	2.500	0.250	0.400	-.150
4	3.000	0.200	0.333	-.133
5	3.500	0.167	0.286	-.119
6	4.000	0.143	0.250	-.107
7	4.500	0.125	0.222	-.097
8	5.000	0.111	0.200	-.089

to construct Figure 12-5.   Error is based on the actual solution.

In Figure 12-6 we list the coordinates of the vertices of the
Euler polygonal approximation to the solution of (4) for various
values of h.   These computations were performed on the CDC 6500
which allows 15 digits in the representation of a real.   Hence, even
though as many as 4,000 points are computed, round off is not a
problem.   Thus, the only errors are due to the method itself.   Y1,
Y01 and Y001 denote the successive values of y obtained by using
an h of 0.1, 0.01 and 0.001, respectively.   YACT denotes the actual
values along the solution.

APPROXIMATE SOLUTIONS OF Y DX + X DY = 0   BY EULERS METHOD

X	Y1	Y01	Y001	YACT
1.000000	1.000000	1.000000	1.000000	1.000000
1.500000	.642857	.664430	.666444	.666667
2.000000	.473684	.497487	.499750	.500000
2.500000	.375000	.397590	.399760	.400000
3.000000	.310345	.331104	.333111	.333333
3.500000	.264706	.283668	.285510	.285714
4.000000	.230769	.248120	.249812	.250000
4.500000	.204545	.220490	.222049	.222222
5.000000	.183673	.198397	.199840	.200000

Figure 12-6

In Section 10 we observed that while the method of upper and lower sums can be used to prove that integrals of uniformly continuous functions exist, it is too crude to be an effective tool for numerically evaluating integrals. In the same way, Euler's method can be shown[1] to converge, as $h \to 0$, to the actual solution to (1) if $\frac{\partial f}{\partial y}$ is continuous. Again, however, it is really too crude a method for effectively approximating the solutions of most differential equations.

The errors in Euler's method are, of course, due to assuming that the solution to (1) is linear over an interval of length h. This is equivalent to assuming that y' is constant over this interval. This is not usually the case, of course. Therefore, our approximate solutions could be improved if, instead of using the slope $y' = f(x_n, y_n)$ over an entire interval, we used some "average" value of the slope over that interval.

One method of doing this is to compute the slope at (X_n, Y_n) and (X_{n+1}, Y_{n+1}) using Euler's method, compute the mean (average) of these slopes and apply this "slope" at (X_n, Y_n). This leads to the formula:

$$(5) \qquad Y_{n+1} = Y_n + h \, \frac{f(X_n, Y_n) + f(X_n + h, \, Y_n + hf(X_n, Y_n))}{2} \; .$$

---

[1]For example, see Calculus, a computer oriented presentation, W. B. Stenberg, R. J. Walker, et al, CRICISAM, 1968.

This recursion formula is known[1] as the <u>Runge-Kutta</u> <u>method</u> <u>of</u> <u>order</u> 2. In Figure 12.7 we exhibit the machine output of the exact solution, YACT, together with the Euler and Runge-Kutta approximations to the solution for the differential equation $y' = -y/x$, $y(1) = 1$.

EULER (YEU) AND RUNGE-KUTTA (YRK) APPROXIMATIONS
TO SOLUTIONS OF Y DX + X DY = 0
(H=.1)

X	YEU	YRK	YACT
1.000000	1.000000	1.000000	1.000000
1.500000	.642857	.666667	.666667
2.000000	.473684	.500000	.500000
2.500000	.375000	.400000	.400000
3.000000	.310345	.333333	.333333
3.500000	.264706	.285714	.285714
4.000000	.230769	.250000	.250000
4.500000	.204545	.222222	.222222
5.000000	.183673	.200000	.200000

Figure 12-7

Other numerical methods of this type are part of the subject matter of texts on numerical analysis[2].

We close this section with a brief description of two other methods of approximating the solutions to differential equations. The first utilizes power series, and the second is an integro-recursive method.

For the first, we recall that if y has derivatives up to order $n + 1$, it may be represented by a Taylor's series:

(6) $\quad y(x) = y(x_0) + y'(x_0)(x-x_0) + \dfrac{y''(x_0)}{2!}(x-x_0)^2 + \dfrac{y'''(x_0)}{3!}(x-x_0)^3 + \cdots$

$$+ \frac{y^{(n)}(x_0)}{n!}(x-x_0)^n + R_{n+1}(x) .$$

Now (1) gives us $y(x_0)$ and $y'(x_0) = f(x_0, y_0)$. If f is differentiable, then we can use (1) to compute

(7) $\qquad\qquad y''(x_0) = f_x(x_0, y_0) + f_y(x_0, y_0)y'(x_0)$

---

[1] See Conte, <u>Numerical</u> <u>Analysis</u>, <u>ibid</u>.

and continuing in this way, compute as many of the coefficients in (6) as the differentiability of f allows. This method is called a Power Series Expansion of the Solutions of (1). Its use is of course restricted to the interval of convergence[1] of (6).

A variant assumes that there is a series solution to (1) of the form

(8) $y = a_0 + a_1 x + a_2 x^2 + a_3 x^3 + \cdots$

This expression is then substituted for y in both members of (1) and simplified to the form of a power series on both sides of the equal sign. Equating the coefficients of the various powers of x and the constant term in the two members gives a recursion formula for the a_n in (8). That is, the process gives a sequence of formulas which give the value of a_n, say, in terms of earlier a_i. Except for relatively simple functions f(x,y), this process can be extremely complicated to apply. A further discussion of the method and its variant is given in most elementary texts on differential equations[2].

The second method requires rewriting (1) in a form called an integral equation. Now,

$$\int_{x_0}^{x} y' = \int_{x_0}^{x} f(x,y(s))\,ds \quad .$$

But,

$$\int_{x_0}^{x} y' = y(x) - y_0 \quad .$$

So,

$$y(x) = y_0 + \int_{x_0}^{x} f(x,y(s))\,ds \quad .$$

---

[1] The right side of (6) may have a meaning only for x in a certain interval containing x_0. This interval is called the interval of convergence. For a further discussion see your calculus text.

[2] For example, see Elements of Ordinary Differential Equations, Golomb and Shanks, McGraw Hill.

The method is to assume an initial form for y, say $y_1(x)$ and generate $y_2(x)$ from:

$$y_2(x) = y_0 + \int_{x_0}^{x} f(s, y_1(s)) \, ds$$

and, finally, apply the recursion formula:

(9) $$y_{n+1}(x) = y_0 + \int_{x_0}^{x} f(s, y_n(s)) \, ds$$

to obtain a sequence of functions $\{y_n(x)\}$ each of which approximates the solution of (1). Under certain assumptions[1], it can be proved that the sequence generated by (9) converges to this solution. The method is known as <u>Picard's Method</u>.

As an example, consider the initial value problem: $y' = y$, $y(0) = 1$. In this case (9) becomes

$$y_{n+1}(x) = 1 + \int_{0}^{x} y_n(s) \, ds \quad.$$

Since we want $y(0) = 1$, it is reasonable to start with $y_1(x) = 1$ which has the correct initial value. Then

$$y_2(x) = 1 + \int_{0}^{x} 1 \, ds = 1 + x$$

and

$$y_3(x) = 1 + \int_{0}^{x} (1 + s) \, ds = 1 + x + \frac{x^2}{2} \quad.$$

$$\vdots$$

$$y_{n+1}(x) = 1 + \int_{0}^{x} \left(1 + s + \frac{s^2}{2!} + \frac{s^3}{3!} + \cdots + \frac{s^{n-1}}{(n-1)!}\right) ds$$

$$= 1 + x + \frac{x^2}{2!} + \frac{x^3}{3!} + \cdots + \frac{x^n}{n!} \quad.$$

---

[1] For example, see <u>Elements</u> of <u>Ordinary</u> <u>Differential</u> <u>Equations</u>, Golomb and Shanks, McGraw Hill.

It will be observed that the polynomial on the right is simply the first n + 1 terms in the Maclaurin expansion of e^x. $y = e^x$ is clearly a solution to the above initial value problem $y' = y$, $y(0) = 1$.

Applying the power series technique to this initial value problem, we observe that since $y' = y$, we have $y'' = y'$, $y''' = y''$, etc. Since $y(0) = 1$ we see that $y = y' = y'' = y''' = \cdots = 1$. Therefore, (6) becomes

$$y = 1 + x + \frac{x^2}{2!} + \frac{x^3}{3!} + \cdots$$

Still other approximate techniques are the subject of courses in Numerical Analysis.

Having completed a brief introduction to the numerical solutions of first order differential equations, we turn our attention to higher order differential equations and to systems of first order equations. We restrict our attention to second order equations of the form:

(10) $$y'' + a(x)y' + b(x)y = 0, \ y(x_0) = y_0, \ y'(x_0) = y_0'$$

though the generalizations to higher order equations will probably be obvious.

By a system of first order differential equations, we mean a pair of interrelated (coupled) equations of the form:

(11) $$\left. \begin{array}{l} y' = f(x,y,u) \\ u' = g(x,y,u) \end{array} \right\} , \ y(x_0) = y_0, \ u(x_0) = u_0$$

where u' means $D_x u$, etc. Of course, this can be generalized to any number of equations.

We first show that we need consider only systems of the form (11) because equations of the form (10) can be reduced to (11). To see this, introduce the notation $y' = u$. Then $y'' = u'$ and (10) can be rewritten:

$$y' = u$$
$$u' = y'' = -(a(x)y' + b(x)y) = -(a(x)u + b(x)y)$$

which is a system of first order equations of the form (11).

Analytic techniques for solving systems such as (11) depend upon ideas studied in courses in linear algebra. However, even without these topics, we may consider numerical solutions by analogy with (2). Euler's form for such systems is:

$$
\begin{matrix}
X_0 = x_0 \\
Y_0 = y_0 \\
U_0 = u_0 \\
Y_n = Y_{n-1} + hf(X_{n-1}, Y_{n-1}, U_{n-1}) \\
U_n = U_{n-1} + hg(X_{n-1}, Y_{n-1}, U_{n-1}) \\
X_n = X_{n-1} + nh
\end{matrix}
\qquad n = 1,2,3,\cdots
$$

(12)

On page 12-128 we noted that it was important that Y_n be computed before X_n. Here, the same caution must be also applied to U_n. FORTRAN statements which accomplish the intention of the last three equations of (12) and minimize the number of variables whose storage is required are:

$$
\begin{aligned}
&YNEW = Y + H*F(X,Y,U) \\
&U = U + H*G(X,Y,U) \\
&Y = YNEW \\
&X = X + H
\end{aligned}
$$

(13)

Runge-Kutta formulas for systems may also be written. The interested reader can find them in a text on Numerical Analysis[1].

EXERCISES

12-1   What are the isoclines of: (a) $y' = x^2 - y^2$,
(b) $y' = 5x^2 - 6xy + 5y^2$,   (c) $y' = y - x^3 + 2x^2 + x - 2$?

12-2   (a) Use the method of isoclines to determine, graphically, the solution to $y' = x^2 - y^2$ which passes through $(2,1)$, i.e., with $y(2) = 1$, (b) Check your graphical result by the Runge-Kutta method.

12-3   Solve $y' = y/2$, $y(0) = 2$, by both Euler and Runge-Kutta methods. Compare with the actual solution.

---

[1]E.g., Conte, _ibid_.

12-4   Use the Runge-Kutta method to solve $y' = -2 + \sqrt{2x + y} - 1$ for the conditions $y(1) = -1$ and for the conditions $y(1) = -.95$. Is your result consistent with Figure 12-3? How do the equations differ?

12-5   Convert $y'' + 3y' + 2y = 0$, $y(0) = 1$, $y'(0) = -1$, to a system and approximate the solution using Euler's method. Compare with the actual solution.

12-6   The equation (A) $y'' + a^2 y = 0$ is derived from the motion of a simple pendulum. A simple analysis shows that this equation should be (B) $y'' + a^2 \sin y = 0$. (Derive this equation.) (A) is said to be the "linearized" approximation to (B). (What justifies this approximation?) Write a recursion relation like (12) for a Runge-Kutta approximation to the solution to (A). Assume $y(0) = 0$, $y'(0) = 1$. Program and run your solution.

12-7   Approximate the solution to $y' = y/2$, $y(0) = 2$ by the method of Taylor series and by Picard's method.

Answers to selected EXERCISES

<u>2-2</u>	Vol = 1.200825E+00 Wgt = 3.866658E-01
<u>2-5</u>	3.036553E-02
<u>3-3</u>	4.028648E+00
<u>3-4</u>	$\sqrt{53.46091}$ = 7.312000E+00
<u>4-2</u>	α = .930799, β = 1.44552, γ = .76528 (in Radians)

<u>4-3</u>   check points (0,1.414214E+00), (9.000000E+00,2.981103E-01)
                  (1.100000E+01,1.002210E+00), (1.300000E+01,1.847854E+00)

<u>5-2</u>,<u>5-3</u>   F(1.800000E+00) = 1.237600E+01

<u>5-5</u>   Some chain lengths: 1:4 (namely: 1,4,2,1); 9:20; 27:112

<u>5-7</u>   Those less than 100 are: (3,5),(5,7),(11,13),(17,19),
                (29,31),(41,43),(59,61),(71,73).

<u>6-1</u>   1.89255E+00

<u>6-3</u> $\sqrt{.5}$ = 7.071078E-01, $\sqrt{75}$ = 8.660260E+00

<u>6-5</u>   Approximate results:
                (a)   2.718 (This limit is e), (c) 1

<u>6-6</u>   2.061769E+00

<u>6-9</u>   Since the computer cannot determine limits, your answer
                can only be approximate. In each case where you can
                suppose a limit exists, this value should be the value
                of the function.

<u>7-3</u> $A = Pe^{rt}$

<u>8-4</u>   See <u>6-5</u>

<u>8-7</u> $.3_{10} \doteq .2314631463_8$

<u>9-1</u>   The first Fibonacci number to exceed 30,000 is the
                24th one 46368.

<u>9-4(b)</u>

THE FUTURE AMOUNT OF $1.00

	INTEREST AT 7. PERCENT COMPOUNDED		
YEAR	SEMIANNUALLY	QUARTERLY	MONTHLY
6	1.511069	1.516443	1.520106

10-1 (a) 8.49153, (b) 8.49244

10-3 (a) $N_R \geq 57{,}422$, $N_T \geq 8$, $N_S \geq 8$ (Since N_S must be even)

(b) $N_R \geq 2{,}500$, $N_T \geq 99$, $N_S \geq 4$ (Since N_S must be even)

(c) $N_R \geq 640{,}000$, $N_T \geq 93$, $N_S \geq 8$ (Since N_S must be even)

10-7 966.8 inches

10-10,10-11 Consult a Table of Logarithms.

10-12 $\sin x \doteq x - \frac{x^3}{3!} + \frac{x^5}{5!} - \frac{x^7}{7!}$, $\cos x \doteq 1 - \frac{x^2}{2!} + \frac{x^4}{4!} - \frac{x^6}{6!} + \frac{x^8}{8!}$

10-13 Consult a Table of values of trigonometric functions.

11-1 (c) (0.590,0.000)

11-2 4.41

11-3

$$m\left\{\begin{array}{ccccccc} \multicolumn{7}{c}{\overbrace{\hspace{4cm}}^{n}} \\ 1 & 2 & 2 & 2 & \cdots & 2 & 1 \\ 2 & 4 & 4 & 4 & \cdots & 4 & 2 \\ 2 & 4 & 4 & 4 & \cdots & 4 & 2 \\ \vdots & & & & & & \\ 2 & 4 & 4 & 4 & \cdots & 4 & 2 \\ 1 & 2 & 2 & 2 & \cdots & 2 & 1 \end{array}\right.$$

11-5 4.94

11-6 When (number of subdivision of height)/(number of subdivisions of circumference)$^2 \to 1$, the "area" is approximately 62.33. When this ratio approaches 5, the "area" is approximately 310.13.

11-12 (a) 2.90, (b) 2.77 (The accuracy can be improved by taking more subdivisions.)

11-13 7.3070

11-16 There are two solutions, approximately: (1.41037,3.06256) (3.12217,1.03030).

12-1 (a) The hyperbolas $x^2 - y^2 = k$

12-3 Actual solution: $y = 2e^{x/2}$

12-5 Actual solution: $y = e^{-x}$

12-7 $y = 2(1 + \frac{x}{2} + \frac{1}{2!}\frac{x^2}{4} + \frac{1}{3!}\frac{x^3}{8} + \frac{1}{4!}\frac{x^4}{16} + \ldots)$

Computer Problems by Topics

Many exercises in calculus texts readily lend themselves to rephrasing for computer applications.

TYPICAL COURSE OUTLINE

This outline is prepared to agree with most of the current texts bearing titles like <u>Calculus, with</u> <u>Analytic</u> <u>Geometry</u>. The expression (Relevant EXERCISES) refers to EXERCISES in this book. The format of the outline is as follows:

Section from this book   (lessons)

    Section from Calculus text (Relevant EXERCISES)   (lessons)

In addition to (Relevant EXERCISES) there are EXERCISES covering the FORTRAN topics. Also included are EXERCISES not related to calculus which provide at once a diversion and a learning experience.

The number of lessons devoted to each section is based on five meetings per week for fifteen weeks. Naturally, this can be varied to meet local needs. Rearrangement of the outline to coincide with the <u>Quarter</u> system will be obvious. The instructor should be aware that computer problems require more lead time than typical text book problems.

First Semester

Introduction to the Computing Center	(1)
Section 1	(2)
Review material through simple aspects of lines	(2)
Section 2	(2)
Analytic Geometry of lines and circles	(2)
Section 3	(1)
Conics	(3)
Section 4	(2)
Functions (4-1,4-3,4-4,5-1)	(1)
Section 5	(2)
Section 6	(2)
Sequences (usually must be taken out of order)	
(3-2,3-3,5-5,6-1,6-4,6-5,8-2,8-3)	(1)
Limits (3-2,3-3,6-1,6-4,6-5,8-2,8-3)	(4)
Differentiation (5-4,8-1)	(11)
Mean Value Theorem and Applications (2-5,3-6,5-8,5-9)	(3)
Section 7	(3)
Applications of derivatives (5-2,5-3,6-7)	(5)

Section 8
    Antiderivatives (3)
    The definite integral (Introduction)
       (8-2,8-3, Section 10) (4)
Section 10 (2)
    The definite integral (Completed) (3)

    Applications of the definite integral (Some
      textbook exercises lead to integral requiring
      numerical approximations) (8)

Section Semester

    Additional applications of the definite integral (5)

    Transcendental Functions (10-10,10-11,10-12,10-13,
      11-7,11-8,11-9) (10)

Section 9A (1)

    Techniques of Integration (14)

    More Analytic Geometry (14)

Section 9B (1)
    Vectors and parametric equations (12)

Section 9C,D (2)
    Indeterminates forms (7)

Section 9E,F (2)

Third Semester (Four meetings per week)

    3-D Analytic Geometry (13)

    Partial differentiation (11-1,11-16) (12)

Section 11A (2)
    Multiple integrals (11-2,11-4,11-5,11-6,11-5,11-12,
      11-13,11-15) (10)

Section 11B,C
    Infinite Series (11-7,11-8,11-9,11-10,11-11,12-7) (12)

Section 11D (3)

Fourth Semester
    Differential Equations

Section 12 (as appropriate)

INDEX

A

Aborted, 1-5
ABS, 4-34
Absolute value, 4-34
Account number, 1-6
Algorithm, 5-39,5-40
Algorithm, infinite, 6-57
ALOG, 4-34
ALOG10, 4-34
Alphameric constants, 9-95
Ap, 9-96
Approximation, 6-52,6-53
   Euler's method, 12-128
   rectangular, 10-104
   Runge-Kutta method, 12-130
   Simpson's rule, 10-105,11-113
   Taylor series, 12-131
   trapezoidal, 10-105,11-112
Arctangent function, 4-34
Argument, 4-34
Arithmetic, symbols of, 2-10
Arithmetic IF, 9-99
Array, 9-86,9-87,9-88
Assignment (statement), 2-12
ATAN, 4-34

B

Base (of number system), 8-75,8-82
Basic FORTRAN, 1-4
Batch processing, 1-5
Bounded sequence, 6-54
Branching, 3-25

C

CALL, 9-94
Card reader, 1-4
Carriage control, 7-68
Center library, 9-95
Character set, 7-62
COMMENT, 2-19
Common logarithm, 4-34
Compiled, 1-4
Compiler, 1-3
Computational instability, 8-77
Compute through, 5-48
Computer Center, 1-4
Consultants, 1-4
Continuation, 2-20
CONTINUE, 9-84
Control cards, 1-5
Control Unit, 1-4
Convergence, 6-53,6-54
COS, 4-34

D

Data card, 1-1
Data deck, 1-5,9-88
Debugging, 1-3,5-48
Deck, 1-1
Diagnostic statement, 1-3,2-11
Differential equations, 12-124
   approximation of solution, 12-126
   first order, 12-124
   system of, 12-134
DIMENSION, 9-86
Direction field, 12-125
Dm.n, 8-81
DO, 9-83
DOUBLE PRECISION, 8-78
   constants, 9-81
   function, 8-81,9-94
Dummy variable, 4-35

E

Em.n, 2-17,7-63
END, 2-20
Error terms (in numerical integration), 10-105
Euler's method, 12-128
   for systems of differential equations, 12-135
Executable statement, 1-4,9-100
Executed, 1-4
Existence theorems, role of, 6-53 10-106,12-124
EXP, 4-34
Exponential function, 4-34
   notation, 2-17
Exponentiation, 2-10,2-15,2-21

F

Family of functions, 4-36
Fibonacci, 6-58
Field specification, 2-17
   description, 7-63
   q identical, 7-65
   width, 7-63
FLOAT, 2-10,4-34
Flowchart, 5-39, 5-41
   examples, 5-43,5-47
   symbols for, 5-41
Fm.n, 7-64
FORMAT, 2-17,7-63,7-67
FORTRAN, 1-3
   integer, 2-13
   real number, 2-13
   statements, 2-20

Calculus with Applications and Computing, Volume 1

by **P. Lax, S. Burstein,** and **A. Lax**
1976. xi, 513p. 170 illus. cloth
Undergraduate Texts in Mathematics

The central theme of this calculus text is the relation of calculus to science. Whole chapters are devoted to single—or several related—scientific topics, teaching the student how the notions of calculus are used to formulate the basic laws of science and how the methods of calculus are used to deduce consequences of those basic laws.

Much emphasis is given to numerical questions. Even when qualitative rather than quantitative understanding is the aim, the calculation of a well-chosen special case can be especially illuminating, taking the role of a crucial experiment in confirming an old speculation, pointing to a new one. So numerical methods are presented in this text as organic parts of calculus, not as a mere list of recipes appended as an afterthought. Computer programs and examples for pocket calculators are included.

Other Undergradute Texts in Mathematics

Apostol: Introduction to Analytic Number Theory
1976. xii, 338 pages.

Chung: Elementary Probability Theory with Stochastic Processes
1975. x, 325 pages. 36 illus.

Croom: Basic Concepts of Algebraic Topology
In preparation.

Fleming: Functions of Several Variables. Second edition
1977. xi, 411 pages. 96 illus.

Halmos: Finite-Dimensional Vector Spaces. Second edition
1974 viii, 200 pages.

Halmos: Naive Set Theory
1974. vii, 104 pages.

Kemeny/Snell: Finite Markov Chains
1976. ix, 210 pages.

LeCuyer: College Mathematics with a Programming Language
In preparation.

Protter/Morrey: A First Course in Real Analysis
1977. xii, 507 pages. 135 illus.

Sigler: Algebra
1976. xii, 419 pages. 32 illus.

Singer/Thorpe: Lecture Notes on Elementary Topology and Geometry
1976. viii, 232 pages. 109 illus.

Smith: Linear Algebra
In preparation.

Springer-Verlag   **New York   Heidelberg   Berlin**

(Micro _____ **CAL**

by **K. L.** _____

1977. ap_____

This text _____ m-solving using
computer _____ e non-numerical
approach _____ l non-science fields.

The book _____ , extended with built-in
functions _____ of the programming
methods _____ examples are
presented _____ hematics "threat"
often felt _____ ith hierarchic
structure _____ the concepts of
structured

Texts _____ iter Science

Chess S _____

Edited by _____

1977. xi, _____

Design of Digital Computers
An Introduction

Second Edition
By **H. W. Gschwind** and **E. J. McCluskey**
1975. ix, 548p. 375 illus. cloth

The Origins of Digital Computers
Selected Papers
Second Edition

Edited by **B. Randell**
1975. xvi, 464p. 120 illus. cloth

Adaptive Information Processing
An Introductory Survey

By **J. R. Sampson**
1976. x, 214p. 83 illus. cloth

Automata-Theoretic Aspects of Formal Power Series

By **A. Salomaa** and **M. Soittola**
1978. approx. 240p. cloth

Springer-Verlag   **New York**   **Heidelberg**   **Berlin**